一天一点英文
Enjoy a Bit of English Everyday

中英双语，全新完美呈现

一天一点英文

盛丹丹/编译

Enjoy a Bit of English Everyday

最寓言·新月海

Zui Fable·New-moon Sea

编委：[美]Alejandro Taylor, George Wen
[英]David Joseph
马凤萍　林彦民　吴桂侠　王立明

大连理工大学出版社
DALIAN UNIVERSITY OF TECHNOLOGY PRESS

图书在版编目(CIP)数据

最寓言·新月海：英汉对照/盛丹丹编译.—大
连：大连理工大学出版社，2010.3(2011.1重印)
（一天一点英文/盛丹丹编译）
ISBN 978-7-5611-5360-4

Ⅰ.①最… Ⅱ.①盛… Ⅲ.①英语—汉语—对照读物
②寓言—作品集—世界 Ⅳ.H319.4：Ⅰ

中国版本图书馆CIP数据核字(2010)第015798号

大连理工大学出版社出版

地址：大连市软件园路80号 邮政编码：116023
发行：0411-84708842 邮购：0411-84703636 传真：0411-84701466
E-mail:dutp@dutp.cn URL:http://www.dutp.cn
辽宁星海彩色印刷有限公司印刷 大连理工大学出版社发行

幅面尺寸：160mm×235mm 印张：17 字数：295千字
印数：5001～8000
2010年3月第1版 2011年1月第2次印刷

责任编辑：张 钰 责任校对：丛倩倩
封面设计：联智昭阳

ISBN 978-7-5611-5360-4 定价：32.00元

写在前面的话
Previous Remark

　　秉着对英语文学的无比敬意和对汉语翻译的深切尊重,我们酝酿并出版了"一天一点英文"中英双语阅读书系,其中包括《最散文·光芒星》、《最小说·天空城》、《最诗歌·灵之翼》、《最童话·梦幻岛》、《最寓言·新月海》、《最幽默·长乐风》六种,力求以点代面综合凸显英语文学的魅力和汉译的艰辛,使亲爱的读者朋友们有种寓学于乐的感觉。《最散文》形散而神不散,行文斑驳而不失寓意;《最小说》风格多样,人物鲜活,描写细腻而情节引人入胜;《最诗歌》追求情调多样、情浓意厚,新颖和经典并存;《最童话》以求索之心唤醒沉睡的童真,故事老少皆宜;《最寓言》每篇短小而深刻,传统道德中融入现代的审美;《最幽默》气氛轻松惬意,让读者在莞尔一笑中增添生活的智慧。

　　在这喧嚣的、快节奏的现代生活中,如果我们能给读者朋友们送去一点点休闲和一点点快乐,那正是我们的心愿,倘若还能多上一点点深刻,我们则求之不得。我们希望此书能成为一部望远镜,把艰难的英文阅读向读者拉近,使之变成一种乐趣。本书系的选材和语言都力求无愧于"最"字,虽然文学之海浩渺无垠、无穷无尽,但是我们坚信,若是读者朋友们能把我们的书系读得通透,定会大受裨益。

　　本书系是整个团队合作的结晶,非常感谢参与丛书编译的全体人员,我们共同的努力协作保证了这套书的质量和品位,我们也期待着来自读者的反馈和意见。

"一天一点英文"书系全体编辑

2010.3

目录
Contents

第一章

处世哲学
Do Things Reasonably

第二章

生存之道
The Point of It All

第三章

智慧箴言
Words of Wisdom

第四章

生活睿语
Life Sagacity

第一章

处世哲学
Do Things Reasonably

The Father and His Quarreling Sons
父亲与争吵的儿子们

A father had a family of sons who were perpetually quarreling among themselves. When he failed to heal their disputes[1] by his exhortations, he was determined to give them a practical illustration[2] of the evil of disunion. And for this purpose one day he told them to bring him a bundle[3] of sticks. When they had done so, he placed the faggot into the hands of each of them in succession, and ordered them to break it into pieces. They tried with all their strength, but they were not able to do it.

He next loosed the faggot, took the sticks separately[4], one by one, and again put them into his sons' hands, upon which they broke them easily. He then addressed them in these words, "My sons, if you are of one mind, and unite to assist each other, you will be like this faggot, uninjured by all the attempts of your enemies; but if you are divided among yourselves, you will be broken as easily as these sticks."

一位父亲有几个孩子,这些孩子时常发生口角。他丝毫没有办法来劝阻他们,只好让他们看看不合群所带来害处的例子。为了达到这个目的,有一天他叫他们替他拿一捆细柴来。当他们把柴带来时,他便先后将那捆柴放在每一个孩子的手中,吩咐他们弄断这捆柴。他们一个个尽力去试,总是不能成功。

然后他解开那捆柴,一根根地放在他们手里,如此一来,他们便毫不费力地折断了。于是他就告诉他们说:"孩子们!如果你们大家团结一致,互相帮助,你们就像这捆柴一样,不能被你们的敌人折断;但如果你们自行分裂,你们就将和这些散柴一般,不堪一折了。"

---

[1] dispute n. 争论

[2] illustration n. 例证,说明

[3] bundle n. 捆,束

[4] separately adv. 分别地

The Ass and His Purchaser[1]
驴和买驴的人

A man wanted to buy an ass. He went to the market, and found a likely one. But he wanted to test him first.

So he took the ass home, and put him into the stable[2] with the other asses. The new ass looked around, and immediately went to a place next to the laziest ass in the stable. When the man saw this, he put a halter on the ass at once, and gave him back to his owner.

The owner felt quite surprised. He asked the man, "Why are you back so soon? Have you tested him already?" "I don't want to test him any more," replied the man, "From the companion he chose for himself, I could see what sort of animal he is."

一个人想到市场上去买头驴子,他看中一头外表不错的驴,但是他想要先试验一下。

他把驴牵回家,放在圈里的其他驴子间。这头新来的驴四处看了看,立即走向圈里一头最好吃懒做的驴旁边。于是,买驴的人立刻给那头驴套上辔头,牵回去还给了卖驴的人。

卖驴的人感到很奇怪,于是问道:"你怎么这么快就回来了? 你已经试好了吗?"买主说:"不必再试了,从他所选择什么样的朋友来看,我已经知道他是什么样了。"

---

[1] purchaser n. 购买者   [2] stable n. 马厩

A Mouse Trap

A mouse looked through a crack in the wall to see the farmer and his wife opening a package. What food might it contain? He was curious, He was aghast[1] to discover that it was a mouse trap!

Retreating[2] to the farmyard, the mouse proclaimed the warning, "There is a mouse trap in the house! There is a mouse trap in the house!" The chicken clucked and scratched, raised her head and said, "Mr. Mouse, I can tell you this is a grave concern to you, but it is of no consequence to me. I cannot be bothered by it." The mouse turned to the pig and told him, "There is a mouse trap in the house!" "I am so sorry, Mr. Mouse," sympathized the pig, "but there is nothing I can do about it but pray; be assured that you are in my prayers." The mouse turned to the cow, who replied, "Like wow, Mr. Mouse, a mouse trap! Am I in grave danger? Haha." With his head down, the mouse was dejected to face the farmer's mouse trap alone.

That very night a sound was heard throughout the house, like a sound of the mouse trap catching its prey. The farmer's wife rushed to see what was caught. In the darkness, she did not see that it was a venomous snake whose tail the trap had caught. The snake bit the farmer's wife. The farmer rushed her to the hospital. She returned home with a fever. Hearing that fresh chicken soup could cure the fever, the farmer took his hatchet[3] to the farmyard for the soup's main ingredient. His wife's sickness continued so that friends and neighbors came to sit with her around the clock. To feed them, the farmer butchered the pig. The farmer's wife did not get well, in fact, she died, and so many people came to her funeral that the farmer had the cow slaughtered[4] to provide meat for all of them to eat.

---

[1] aghast adj. 吃惊的，吓呆的

[2] retreat v. 撤退，退却

[3] hatchet n. 短柄小斧

[4] slaughter v. 屠杀(牲口)

一只鼠夹

一只老鼠从墙上的缝隙里向屋里窥视，发现农夫和妻子正在打开一个包裹。包里是什么好吃的呢？老鼠很好奇。结果他惊恐地发现里面竟是个鼠夹！

他赶忙溜了出来，来到院子里宣布这个可怕的消息。"屋里有只鼠夹！屋里有只鼠夹！"母鸡听到后咯咯大笑，她一边用爪子挠着地面，一边高昂着头说道："老鼠先生，我可以告诉你，它对你来说是个性命攸关的问题，但是对于我又有什么关系呢？我可不会被它影响的。"老鼠转向猪说："屋里有个鼠夹！""对此我深表遗憾，老鼠先生，"猪同情地说，"但是除了祈祷我也没有其他的办法，希望我的祈祷能保佑你。"老鼠又向奶牛诉说了这个消息。奶牛回答道："什么？一个鼠夹！老鼠先生，难道对我是什么致命的威胁吗？哈哈。"老鼠只好垂头丧气地回到屋里，沮丧地独自面对这个可怕的东西——鼠夹。

就在那天晚上，屋里传来了响声，听起来像是鼠夹捕获了猎物。农夫的妻子冲到那里去看什么被逮住了。黑暗中，她没看清夹子夹住了一条毒蛇的尾巴。这时，毒蛇狠狠地咬了她一口。农夫赶忙把妻子送到医院，回来后她就一直高烧不退。听说新鲜的鸡汤能治病，于是农夫拿着斧子来到院子里杀了母鸡。但是妻子的病情仍未见好转，周围的邻居和朋友们都来看望她。为了招待他们，农夫又杀了猪。后来，妻子的病不治而亡。许多人来参加她的葬礼，农夫只好又让人宰了奶牛来招待他们。

Chopsticks

A woman who had worked all her life to bring about good was granted one wish: "Before I die, let me visit both hell and heaven."

Her wish was granted.

She was whisked off to a great banqueting hall. The tables were piled high with delicious food and drink. Around the tables, sat miserable, starving[1] people as wretched[2] as could be. "Why are they like this?" she asked the angle who accompanied her. "Look at their arms." the angel replied. She looked and saw that attached to the people's arms were long chopsticks secured above the elbows[3]. Unable to bend their elbows, the people aimed the chopsticks at the food, but missed every time and sat hungry, frustrated[4] and miserable. "Is this indeed hell? Take me away from here!"

She was then whisked off to heaven. Again she found herself in a great banqueting hall with delicious food piled high on the tables. Around the tables sat people laughing, contented, and joyful. "No chopsticks here, I suppose." she said.

"Oh, yes. There are. Look, just as in hell they are long and attached above the elbows, but look... here people have learnt to feed one another."

[1] starve v. 挨饿　　　　　　　　[3] elbow n. 肘
[2] wretched adj. 可怜的, 不幸的　　[4] frustrated adj. 失意的, 泄气的

筷子

一个终生勤苦行善的女人被允许实现一个愿望："在我死之前,让我参观一下天堂和地狱。"

终于她如愿以偿。

她被带到一间宴会大厅。桌子上堆满了可口的饭菜和饮品。一群人围桌而坐,痛苦不堪,饥饿至极,看上去十分可怜。"他们为什么会这样?"她问同她一起来的天使。"你看他们的胳膊。"天使回答道。她看过之后才明白,他们的胳膊肘部以上都被筷子固定住了。由于肘部不能弯曲,虽然他们的筷子都朝着饭菜伸去却每次都以失败告终,只能饿着肚子沮丧而又痛苦地坐在这里。"这难道就是地狱?请带我离开这儿吧。"

然后她被带到了天堂。在那儿,她也看见了一间宴会大厅,里面有盛满丰盛饭菜的餐桌。围桌而坐的人们却是笑声朗朗,显得高兴而且满足。"我猜这儿没有筷子了吧?"她说。

"哦,不,这儿也有。看,就像地狱中的人们一样,也有筷子绑在他们的胳膊肘上,但是再看……这儿的人们学会了如何去给别人喂饭。"

The Big Crab and the Little Crab
大螃蟹和小螃蟹

A little crab was crawling[1] sideways awkwardly[2]. A big crab sitting by the rock saw him and asked, "My little friend, where are you heading? To the north, the south, the east, or the west?"

"I just want to go to the pond." said the little crab breathlessly.

"Then isn't it easier for you to go straight?" said the big crab. "If you crawl sideways like this, I'm afraid you can't make it there!"

The little crab said, "Well, will you be so kind as to show me how to walk straight?"

The big crab started to demonstrate[3] that but failed to do so no matter how hard he tried. The little crab said, "Forget it! It seems I'll have to keep on crawling sideways, as the biggest member in our family can't even make it straight!"

一只小螃蟹正笨拙地横着爬行。坐在石头旁边的大螃蟹看见了,问他:"我的小朋友,你究竟是想到哪去呢? 是去北面? 南面? 东面还是西面?"

"我只是想到池塘里去。"小螃蟹气喘吁吁地说道。

"那你径直向前走过去,不是容易得多吗?"大螃蟹说,"你再这么横着爬,我怕你永远也爬不到那里呢。"

小螃蟹说:"好吧,那么你能给我做个示范,怎么样直着向前爬吗?"

大螃蟹开始给他示范了,可是他怎么试也不行。小螃蟹说道:"算啦! 看样子我还是要横着爬了,因为我们家族最大的螃蟹都无法直着向前走呢!"

---

[1] crawl v. 爬,爬行

[2] awkwardly adv. 笨拙地,困难地

[3] demonstrate v. 论证,证明,证实

The Donkey and the Frog
驴和青蛙

One day, a donkey was carrying a bundle[1] of wood and walking along the road. When he was crossing a pond, he fell into it incautiously. He struggled to come out from the water but in vain[2]. The donkey moaned and cried for help.

Some frogs living in the water heard the cries. They came to the donkey in crowd and derided, "You only fell into the river once and you make such a fuss[3]. How about us who stay in the water for such a long time? How painful would you be if you were in our position?"

有一天，一只驴驮着木材，一路向前走着。当他经过一个池塘时，一不小心，摔进了池塘里，他挣扎着却总是无法爬上岸来。驴子便唉声叹气地高呼救命。

住在池塘里的青蛙听见了驴的呼救声，成群出来围观。青蛙对驴讥讽说："你只不过是摔了一跤，跌进池塘里，就这样大嚷大叫，高喊救命，如果你像我们一样长期居住在这里，你又会痛苦成什么样子呢？"

---

[1] bundle n. 一捆，一束

[2] vain adj. 徒劳的，无结果的

[3] fuss n. 大惊小怪，小题大做

The Donkey and the Sacred[1] Statue[2]

Once upon a time, a sculptor made a sacred statue, and wanted to send it to the temple in town. He put the statue on the back of a donkey. The donkey then followed a procession to the temple.

Along the way, the sculptor took good care of the donkey that carried the statue, and always cleared the way for him, fearing that he would rush into something.

When the procession reached the town, the people of the town bowed[3] respectfully[4] to the statue.

The donkey that was carrying the statue thought that the people were bowing to him. "Oh, I am well respected!" thought the donkey conceitedly. "That is why they are bowing respectfully to me."

He felt very proud. He began to bray to show how happy he was.

When the town people heard the braying of the donkey, they said, "How can a donkey that carries the sacred statue behave so badly?"

The sculptor at once knew what the donkey was thinking about. He felt very embarrassed and shouted angrily at the donkey, "They were bowing respectfully to the statue, not to you!"

---

[1] sacred adj. 神圣的

[2] statue n. 雕像

[3] bow v. 低头，鞠躬

[4] respectfully adv. 恭敬地

驴和神像

从前，有个雕刻师，雕好了一座圣像，准备将它送往城里的圣堂内。他把圣像放在一只驴的背上，让驴驮着。然后这只驴跟着一列队伍浩浩荡荡地朝圣堂走去。

一路上，雕刻师格外关心驮圣像的驴，总是小心翼翼地为他开路，生怕他撞到什么东西。

他们进到城里时，城里的人们见到圣像，都很虔诚地鞠躬。

驮着神像的驴认为人们在向他鞠躬，洋洋得意地想："看，我是多么地受人尊敬啊！不然人们怎么会向我恭敬地鞠躬呢。"

他感到无比地自豪，他嘶叫着表达自己的喜悦。

城里的人们听到了驴子的嘶叫，说道："怎么能让这么一头没有教养的驴来驮高贵的圣像？"

雕刻师马上知道驴心里想的是什么，他感到非常尴尬，于是生气地向驴大喊："人们只是在向圣像膜拜，还轮不到你！"

The War-horses Turning the Mill

Once upon a time, there was a king who trained many strong and powerful war-horses. The ruler[1] of a neighboring country, who had planned to conquer[2] his land, gave up the idea when he heard that the king had a lot of good horses.

The king was happy to know that his neighbor would not be declaring war on him. He thought, " I trained those war-horses to resist the aggression of the neighboring countries. Since they didn't dare to do so, what is the use of keeping the horses any more?"

Thus he ordered that the eyes of the horses be covered and sent the horses to turn the mills[3] to earn more income for the country, besides earn livings by themselves.

Some years later, the ambitious ruler of the neighboring country had trained his army and horses to try to invade the king's country.

Now the king realized the use of those horses and quickly ordered the war-horses to be sent to the battlefield to defend the country.

The warriors rode on the horses, trying to charge at the enemies, but the horses now only knew how to turn round and round on the same spot. After so many years of turning the mill, the war-horses had forgotten how to charge at their enemies. Seeing that, their enemies got together to charge at them and won the war easily.

[1] ruler n. 统治者,管辖者

[2] conquer v. 占领,击败

[3] mill n. 磨坊,碾磨机

战马推磨

从前，有个国王驯养了很多身体强壮的战马。邻国的国王本想发动战争，侵占他的领土，但是一听说这个国王有许多良马，就放弃了侵占这个念头。

国王听到邻国不战自退的消息，很是高兴。他想："我驯养战马的目的，是为了抵抗邻国的侵略，既然现在邻国不敢侵略我们了，驯养这些战马还有什么用呢？"

于是，国王下令，把所有的战马的眼睛蒙起来，让它们挑起推磨的工作。这样一来，战马不但可以自食其力，还可以增加国家收入。

多年以后，心怀不轨的邻国统治者精心训练了士兵和战马，再次对这个国王的国家发起了侵略战争。

这时候，国王想起了战马的用处，立即下令，赶快让战马披挂上阵。

勇士们骑在战马上，试图冲向敌军阵营，可惜这些战马由于常年推磨碾米的缘故，到了战场上只会原地转圈儿，却不向前冲锋。敌人见状，一起杀过来，轻而易举地打败了国王的军队。

Life Is a Do-it-yourself Project

An elderly carpenter was ready to retire. He told his employer his plans to leave the house-building business and live a more leisurely[1] life with his wife, enjoying his extended family. He would miss the paycheck, but he needed to retire. They could get by.

The employer was sorry to see his good worker go and asked if he could build just one more house as a personal favor. The carpenter said yes, but in time it was easy to see that his heart was not in his work. He resorted to shoddy workmanship and used inferior[2] materials. It was an unfortunate way to end his house-building career.

When the carpenter finished his work and the employer came to inspect the house and handed the front-door key to the carpenter. "This is your house," he said, "my gift to you."

What a shock! What a shame! If he had only known he was building his own house, he would have done it all differently. Now he had to live in the house he had built none too well.

So it is with us. We build our lives in a distracted way, reacting rather than acting, willing to put up less than the best. At important points we do not give the job our best effort. Then with a shock we look at the situation we have created and find that we are now living in the house we have built. If we had realized, we would have done it differently.

Think of yourself as the carpenter. Think about your house. Each day you hammer a nail, place a board, or erect a wall. Build it wisely. It is the only life you will ever build. Even if you live it for only one day more, that day deserves to be lived graciously[3] and with dignity. The plaque[4] on the wall says, "Life is a do-it-yourself project." Who could say it more clearly? Your life tomorrow will be the result of your attitudes and the choices you make today.

打造自己的生活

一位上了年纪的木匠做好了退休的准备。他告诉老板他准备离开建筑行业，与老伴和儿孙们一起共享天伦之乐，过一种更悠闲自得的生活。虽然他因此而少了份薪水，但他想退休了。至于日子嘛，还可以凑合着过。

眼看这位优秀的木匠就要离去，老板很遗憾。他问木匠可否帮忙再建一所房子。木匠答应了，可明眼人一眼就看得出来，此时他做事心不在焉，做出的活儿技艺粗糙，用的料也没那么讲究了。他就这样为自己的建筑生涯划上了句号，真是令人遗憾。

房子建好后，老板过来看房子并交给木匠一把前门钥匙，说："这房子归你了，是我送给你的礼物。"

多么让人吃惊，多么让人羞愧啊！假如他知道他是在为自己造房，他会做得大不一样。现在他不得不住在自己建造的那所粗制滥造的房子里了。

我们又何尝不是如此呢？我们心浮气躁地打造生活，不是主动工作而是被动应付，能省事就省事。关键的时候也没尽心尽力。蓦然回首，才瞠目结舌地发现自己正住在自己建造的那所房子中，自食苦果。早知如此，何必当初。

就当你自己就是那位木匠吧。就当你为自己建房，每天要钉钉、铺板、砌墙。那么，你就该用心地去建。这是你建造的惟一生活。哪怕你只在房子里多生活一天，这一天也应该活得优雅、有尊严。墙上的铭匾写道："生活正如一项为自己打造的工程。"还有什么比这更清楚的呢？明日的生活之果，孕育于你今天的态度和抉择之上。

---

[1] leisurely adj. 悠闲的，不慌不忙的

[2] inferior adj. 差的，次的

[3] graciously adv. 优雅地，和蔼地，慈祥地

[4] plaque n. 匾，名牌，饰板

The North Wind and the Sun

The north wind and the sun were good friends. One day, they were quarrelling[1] over who was more powerful.

The north wind said, "Of course I'm more powerful. Just a gentle blow will make everybody shiver all over with cold."

The sun said, "Oh no, I'm more powerful. I just heat myself up a little bit and everybody will be sweating in no time."

At this moment, a man passed by. The north wind suggested, "Let's see who of us can make him take off his coat. That one is the more powerful!" The sun agreed.

The north wind started off by blowing out a breath of air slowly. The man felt cold and buttoned up his coat. The north wind took a deeper breath and blew harder. The man felt colder. He pulled the coat closer instead of taking it off. He even held the collar[2] up against the bitter wind.

The north wind was furious. This time around he blew with all his strength. The man couldn't stand the chill[3]. He tried to shrink into the coat and folded his arms on his chest. He was tugging[4] the coat even closer to his body. The north wind finally conceded[5] defeat.

The sun sneered and said, "Now, brother wind, let me show you something."

He brushed away the cloud and shone all over. The sunlight drove away the chill and the man suddenly felt warm. He unfolded his arms, turned the collar down and unbuttoned his coat.

The sun worked harder to produce more heat and light. The man, sweating all over now, removed his coat at once. As the sunshine burning he started to strip[6] himself and jumped into the river nearby to cool off.

And the winner was the sun!

北风和太阳

北风和太阳是好朋友,有一天,他们为争论谁的本领大而吵[1]了起来。

北风说:"当然是我的本领大。我只要轻轻一吹,所有人都会冻得浑身发抖。"

太阳说:"不可能,我的本领大,我只要稍稍一变热,人们全都立刻热得出汗。"

这时,有个行人恰好经过。北风说:"我们来比一比,看谁能让这个人把外套脱下来,就算谁的本领大。"太阳同意了。

于是,北风开始慢慢地吹出了一口气。行人忽然觉得很冷,于是把原来敞开的衣服扣紧。北风不服,他深深地吸了一口气,鼓起腮帮子用力一吹。行人觉得更冷了,不但没有脱去衣服,反而把衣服裹得更紧,还把衣领[2]竖起来抵挡寒风。

北风气坏了,他用尽全身力气一吹。行人受不了这种寒冷[3],缩起了脖子,把双臂抱在胸前,反而把衣服裹得更密实了。最后,北风不得不认输了。

太阳讥讽道:"北风小弟,你还是瞧瞧我的本领吧。"

太阳从云层中走出,他用力一照,温暖的光芒驱散了寒冷。行人突然感到热了,他伸开双臂,放下衣领,解开衣扣。

太阳再度使劲发出更多光和热,行人现在浑身是汗,马上脱下了外套。可是阳光越来越猛烈,行人不得不脱光衣服[6],跳进了附近的小河来躲避酷热的太阳。

太阳大获全胜。

---

[1] quarrel v. 争吵,吵架

[2] collar n. 衣领

[3] chill n. 寒冷

[4] tug v. 猛拉,猛拽

[5] concede v. 不情愿地承认

[6] strip v. 脱光衣服

The Camel and the Fox
骆驼和狐狸

A camel was crossing the river, and there was a fox watching from the opposite riverbank.

When the camel got up the riverbank, the fox asked, "Is the water deep?"

The camel said, "Not so. The shallow[1] area is as high as the ankles and the deepest area is only up to the height of the knees."

The fox was relieved to hear that and he started to cross the river, walking towards the opposite[2] riverbank.

However, before he reached the middle of the river, the water level was already up to his chest[3]. He cried, "Liar! I thought you said the deepest area is only up to the knees. Why is the water so deep after a few steps?"

The camel looked at the struggling fox in the river and said, "That depends on whose knees!"

一只骆驼涉水过河,对岸有一只狐狸正看着他。

骆驼上了岸,狐狸问:"水深吗?"

骆驼说:"不深,浅的地方只到我的脚踝;最深的地方才到膝盖。"

狐狸听了骆驼的话,便放心地下了河,向对岸走去。

不料,狐狸还没走到河中央,水就已淹到他的胸膛。他大声喊起来:"骗子!你明明说最深的地方才到膝盖,怎么刚下河没走几步就这么深了?"

骆驼对着正在河中央挣扎的狐狸说:"那可得看是谁的膝盖呀!"

---

[1] shallow adj. 浅的
[2] opposite adj. 相反的,对面的
[3] chest n. 胸部

Sowing Seeds from a Sedan Chair
蠢人种地

A man once came to the field where he saw some lushly[1] grown wheat. He asked the farmer, "How do you grow the wheat so well?"

The farmer said, "Plough[2] the land with frequent applications of fertilizer[3] to make wheat grow well."

The man followed the farmer's advice, but he worried that he would step on the land and damage the soil, causing the wheat couldn't grow from the soil. He therefore hired four workers to carry him on a sedan chair while he sowed the seeds. In this way, he wouldn't step on the land.

Little did he realize that while he prevented his two feet from stepping on the land, he had a total of eight feet stepping on it, which damaged the soil even more!

从前有个人来到田里,见到麦苗长得很茂盛,便问农夫:"你是怎么使麦子长得这么好的?"

农夫说:"把土地翻松,还要勤施肥,这样就可以使麦子长得好了。"

那人便按农夫的说法去种麦子,可又怕自己的脚踩坏了土地,导致麦苗无法从土中生长出来,便坐在轿子上,雇用四个人抬着他,他则坐在上面播种,这样就踩不到地了。

这个人不知道因为怕自己的两只脚踩地而雇用四个人抬着他,最终却导致八只脚踩地,反而把地踩得更结实了。

---

[1] lushly adv. 繁荣地,丰富地,茂盛地　　[3] fertilizer n. 肥料,化肥
[2] plough v. 犁地

The Suspicious[1] Pigeon

There was a pair of pigeons, a male and a female, who pooled[2] their efforts to collect plenty of barley and wheat. They stored the grain in their nest to serve as food in the winter. When summer came, the weather was very hot and dry. The moisture content of the grain was reduced due to evaporation, causing seemly reduction in volume[3].

It appeared to be so much less that the male pigeon became suspicious of the female pigeon. He thought that the female pigeon had stolen some of the grain.

"Have you taken some of the grain?" he asked the female pigeon directly.

"No, I swear I have not taken even a single one."

The male pigeon did not believe her. He beat her with his wings and pecked her to death.

After summer, the weather turned cooler. As the air turned humid, the grain in the store absorbed the moisture and its volume increased. Finally, the grain resumed the original volume.

The male pigeon stared at the grain and suddenly realized what had really happened. He had killed the innocent female pigeon! He was so remorseful that he lay beside the female pigeon's body and mourned. The more he thought of the incident, the more sorrowful he became. In the end, he died of hunger as he did not eat or drink for many days.

---

[1] suspicious adj. 怀疑的, 疑心的　　　　[3] volume n. 体积, 容积

[2] pool v. 把(物品)集中使用

起疑心的鸽子

有一对鸽子,一只雄的和一只雌的。他们一起收集了许多大麦和小麦,并把它们储藏在树上的窝里,准备作为冬天的食物。到了夏天,气候炎热干燥,麦子里的水分蒸发了,因此麦子收缩,麦堆的体积也相应地缩小了,看上去数量好像减少了。

由于数量减少得太多,雄鸽子对雌鸽子起了疑心,认为是雌鸽子偷吃了麦子。

"是你偷吃了麦子吗?"雄鸽子直截了当地问雌鸽子。

"不,我发誓,我一粒也没有吃过。"

雄鸽子不相信,用翅膀打她,用嘴啄她,一直到把她给折磨死了为止。

夏天过去了,气候转凉,空气变得湿润,窝里储藏的麦子吸入了湿气而渐渐膨胀。最后,麦堆又恢复了原来的体积。

雄鸽子看到这样的情况,才恍然大悟,知道雌鸽子已无辜地被自己虐杀了,心里百般懊悔,便躺在死去的雌鸽子身旁叹息,越想越伤心,多日来不吃不喝。后来终于也死去了。

The Impatient Colt

A train of carts with pots moves slowly on in line. The road falls steep and straight, so leaving all the rest upon the top to wait, the driver guides the first down the sharp incline. The good horse almost bears all the weight upon his spine to let the quick, revolving wheels stop. A colt, still waiting on the top, pours out at every step a flood of empty prate.

"Now, there's a charger! Does he look like it? He sticks there like a crab[1]! First rate! Look there! He nearly hit that stone! Oh lord, how crooked! He should have gone to left, that's plain. Step out! Now, there he jolts[2] again! A simple donkey! Uphill, yes, all right, or if it were by night, he can be understood. But all downhill, in an open day! It drives me wild, so poor a show. Best carry water-butts, if that is all you know! You see me sweeping down! I'll show the way! No fear! No lagging behind! There shall not be any lagging! We'll see it's rolling with our cart-not dragging!"

And now he's arched his back, stretches his chest, and sets his cart agoing[3] like the wind. He makes a dash and scampers like the wind; the cart begins to sway and presses close behind, jolts him on the back, and jerks him on the side. He breaks away, and gallops down in full strides. How jolly! Each stone, each crevice, and there comes a bump, a thump! Left, left! The cart goes smashed into the gully[4], and master's pots, away the jump!

[1] crab n. 螃蟹

[2] jolt v. 摇晃

[3] agoing adv. 正在运行中,运转地

[4] gully n. 峡谷

心急的小雄马

一些载有罐子的马车纵队慢行着。路突然变得陡峭而笔直。车夫把其余的车留在山顶等待,赶着第一辆车沿着陡坡下行。那匹驯良的马用他的脊梁承受着几乎全车的重量,好让那快速旋转的车轮停下来。一匹仍在山顶等待的小雄马每挪动一步就喋喋不休地说一堆废话。

"这就是那头很棒的马!怎么不像啊?粘在那里像一只螃蟹!一流的速度!看那儿!他快要碰到那块石头了!哦,上帝!这个不老实的家伙!应该往左拐,那边是平地。快跑啊!看,他又开始摇摇晃晃了!一头蠢驴!要是上山,或者在夜里还情有可原,可现在是下山,是白天呀!我都要疯了,这是一场多么蹩脚的表演啊!如果干不了这活儿还不如去驮水桶呢!你看我几乎是飞奔而下!看我来领路,无所畏惧!绝不会落后!绝不拖拖拉拉!保管车子飞驰而下!"

于是,他躬起背,挺起胸,拉起马车,风驰电掣般地猛冲下去。马车开始摇晃,从后面紧逼上来,撞到他的背部,磕碰到他的两肋。他迈开大步,奔驰而下,多痛快!撞每一块岩石,每一条岩缝,都发出砰、嘭的声音。往左,往左!车子轰隆一声坠入山谷,主人的罐子也摔得到处飞!

The Good Cat
好猫

There was a man who hated rats very much. His house happened to be plagued[1] by rats. They ran all over the place and were bold enough even to jump onto the stove during the daytime.

The man finally paid a lot of money for a good cat that would get rid of the rats. The cat was really beautiful, with long pure white fur. It was also chubby and adorable. The man fed it with sumptuous[2] meat and fish, and let it sleep on the carpet.

As the cat was given good food and a cosy[3] bed every day, it was not keen on catching rats at all. The cat even fooled around with the rats. Hence, the rats became more rampant[4] and fearless.

The cat's master became so furious that he sent the cat away. He swore never to keep cats anymore. And he believed that there was no such a thing as a good cat on earth!

有一个人非常讨厌老鼠,可是家里却闹起了鼠灾,老鼠满屋子跑来跑去,甚至连大白天都敢跳到灶台上。

于是,这个人花重金买来了一只很善于捕鼠的好猫。这只猫漂亮极了,白白的长毛没有一根杂毛,胖胖的身躯很逗人喜爱。那人用鲜美的大鱼大肉喂它,让它睡在地毯上。

猫每天吃得好,住得又舒适,就不再去抓老鼠了,甚至,它还和老鼠一起嬉戏。这样,老鼠就更加肆无忌惮,闹得更凶了。

猫的主人非常恼怒,把猫送走了,并发誓从此再不养猫了。他还因此而认为天下根本就没有好猫。

---

[1] plague v. 使染瘟疫,使受灾祸

[2] sumptuous adj. 豪华的,奢侈的

[3] cosy adj. 温暖舒适的

[4] rampant adj. 猖獗的,不可控制的

The Farmer and the Eagle
农夫和老鹰

A farmer found an eagle caught in the trap[1] which was set by the hunter on his way home. As the eagle was struggling in great pain, the farmer went up to set him free. As the eagle was saved, he was very grateful to the farmer.

One day, the farmer was taking a rest beside a wall after he finished his work. However, he didn't know that the wall was going to fall down.

The eagle found the farmer was in danger, so he took away the farmer's headdress[2] and flew away. To get back his headdress, the farmer got up and ran after the eagle. The eagle dropped the headdress, when he saw the farmer was away from the wall.

As the farmer bent over to pick up his headdress, he heard a big sound. When he turned around, he saw the wall he leaned on fall down. At that time, he realized the eagle came to save his life.

一个农夫在他回家的路上发现了一只陷入了猎人陷阱的老鹰。看到老鹰在那里痛苦地挣扎,农夫走上前将它放了。获得了自由的老鹰对农夫感激不尽。

有一天,这个农夫干完了地里的农活之后靠在一堵墙上休息,但他不知道身后的这堵墙要塌了。

老鹰发现了农夫正身处险境,于是它叼起农夫的头巾,向远处飞去。农夫赶忙起身去追回他的头巾。当老鹰看到农夫已经离开了那堵墙的时候,它松开了叼在嘴里的头巾。

当农夫弯腰拾起他的头巾的时候,听到一声巨响。他转身一看,原来是刚才他倚靠的那堵墙倒塌了。这时,他才明白老鹰是赶来救他的命的。

---

[1] trap n. 陷阱,捕捉器   [2] headdress n. 头饰,头巾

The Crow and the Magpie[1]

A crow in the southern part of a small country had just hatched a baby. The mother crow took great care of her young baby. Soon the baby became fully-fledged[2], and the mother wanted to teach her baby how to chirp[3].

The mother crow thought, "My voice doesn't sound nice, and everybody hates me for that. If I can't do anything about it, why not let my baby have a chance to make a change!"

Therefore, the mother crow took her baby to see a magpie. She said, "My son is a crow but I would like him to sound like you. I hope you will be my son's teacher. Please don't reject. In the future, when he can get rid of his harsh voice and acquire a sweet one, everybody in the world will start admitting him instead of condemning[4] him. I will definitely remember your good deeds and repay your kindness in some way."

The magpie finally accepted the baby crow and started to teach him how to chirp. At first, the magpie patiently taught the baby crow; as time went by, he showed no change at all, and the magpie couldn't stand any more. Finally, the magpie lost his temper. He pecked the baby crow and hit him with his claws, then the baby crow couldn't endure the misery.

Then the magpie looked at the baby crow thoughtfully, and said, "Of course, you're born a crow, and I can't possibly change the way you sound!" Then the magpie sent him home.

When the baby crow returned home and saw his mother, both of them started to cry, in perfect harmony—the way that crows are supposed to sound.

---

[1] magpie n. 喜鹊

[2] fully-fledged adj. 受过充分训练的, 羽翼丰满的

[3] chirp v. （小鸟或某些昆虫）发出的唧唧声

[4] condemn v. 斥责, 谴责

乌鸦和喜鹊

在一个小国家的南方,有一只乌鸦,刚孵化出一只小乌鸦。乌鸦妈妈细心地养育着小乌鸦。不久,小乌鸦羽毛长全了,乌鸦妈妈准备教他鸣叫。

乌鸦妈妈心想:"我的声音不好听,世上的人都因此讨厌我。而我惟一能做的事情就是让我的儿子有个改变嗓音的机会!"

于是,乌鸦妈妈带着小乌鸦去拜见喜鹊,说:"我的儿子虽然是只乌鸦,但是我却想让他学您的叫声。希望您当我的儿子的老师,不要拒绝。如果我儿子的叫声从不好听转变为好听,如果世上的人对我的儿子的叫声从讨厌转变为喜欢,到那时我肯定不能忘记您的恩惠,一定报答您。"

喜鹊终于接受了小乌鸦,并开始教他鸣叫。最初喜鹊还是很有耐性,可是随着日子一天天地流逝,小乌鸦发出的还是哑哑声,喜鹊实在忍无可忍。最后,他禁不住发火了,用嘴啄小乌鸦,还用爪子打他。小乌鸦再也受不了这种苦楚。

于是,喜鹊看着小乌鸦,若有所悟,说:"你本是乌鸦种族,我实在是没有办法可以改变你的叫声!"然后便打发他回去了。

小乌鸦回到他的巢,见到了乌鸦妈妈——两只乌鸦哑哑叫,非常和谐动听——这才是他们本该发出的叫声。

The Fox and the Cockerel

A Fox was prowling[1] round a farmyard one day when he saw a Cockerel standing on a grassy mound[2].

"I've never seen such a handsome bird as you." said the Fox, "Except your father, of course. I used to know him well. What a good voice he had. I don't suppose I'll ever hear anything like that again."

The Cockerel preened[3] his feathers.

"People say I have quite a good voice." he said modestly[4], "Perhaps you would like to hear it and see if it is as good as my father's."

"Yes, please." said the Fox, turning away to lick his lips.

The Cockerel stretched himself to his full height, closed his eyes tight and began to crow at the top of his voice. At once, the Fox grabbed him by the neck and ran off with him into the field.

"Stop, thief!" shouted some men who were working there.

"Give us back that Cockerel." The men began to run after the Fox.

"If I were you," said the Cockerel, turning his head round to talk to the Fox. "I would tell them to mind their own business. Tell them I belong to you and they will stop chasing you."

The Fox opened his mouth to call out, and the Cockerel flew as fast as he could to the top of the tallest tree in sight.

"Why didn't I keep my mouth shut?" the Fox blamed himself angrily.

"That was a lucky escape." thought the Cockerel, "I'll keep my eyes open in future."

---

[1] prowl v. 偷偷潜行, 悄悄走动

[2] mound n. 土堆, 土丘

[3] preen v. （鸟）用嘴梳理（羽毛）

[4] modestly adv. 谦逊地, 谨慎地

狐狸和公鸡

一天，一只狐狸在农场附近徘徊，看到一只公鸡站在长满草的土丘上。

"我从来没见过像你这般俊俏的禽类，"狐狸说，"当然，除了你父亲外。我过去和他很熟，他有一副好嗓子。我想，再也听不到那么美妙的声音了。"

公鸡用嘴梳理了一下身上的羽毛。

"人们说我的嗓子的确不错，"他谦逊地说，"你不妨听一下，听听是不是和我父亲的一样好。"

"好啊，请吧。"狐狸说着，转过头去舔了舔嘴。

公鸡挺直了身子，紧闭双眼，开始放声高歌。狐狸立刻咬住他的脖子向田里跑去。

"小偷！站住！"在地里干活的人喊道。

"把我们的公鸡还回来。"人们开始追赶狐狸。

"如果我是你，"公鸡扭过头对狐狸说，"我会告诉他们不要多管闲事，告诉他们我属于你，他们就不会追赶你了。"

狐狸张开嘴大喊，而公鸡快速飞到眼前最高的树梢上。

"为什么我不一直闭着嘴呢?"狐狸气愤地自责道。

"真是死里逃生，"公鸡想，"以后我得睁大眼睛了。"

Two Mice Drink the Milk
老鼠喝奶

One day, there were two hungry mice who went out of their home looking for food. They found one big pot filled with tasty milk. In order to taste the milk, one of them came up with an idea. One mouse would climb up the pot on the other's back. He would then hold on to the rim[1] of the pot while the other held on to his tail. The first mouse would then descend[2] into the pot to drink the milk without falling into it.

While the first mouse was drinking the milk as planned, the second one was disatisfied.

While the first mouse was drinking without an end, the second mouse became impatient[3]; he shouted, "Enough! It's my turn now!" As the second mouse opened his mouth, he let go of the first mouse's tail. The first mouse fell into the milk pot and soon drowned.

At this time, the second mouse happily thought, "Fine, now that he is drowned, I can have the milk all myself." He began circling the pot but could not find a way to climb up to the pot. Finally he starved to death.

有一天,两只饥肠辘辘的老鼠结伴出洞去找食物。他们发现了一口大锅,里面盛着香喷喷的牛奶。为了能尝到锅中的牛奶,其中一只老鼠想出了一个主意——其中的一只老鼠可以踩着另一只的背爬到锅上。这样他可以把着锅沿,另一只拽着他的尾巴。第一只老鼠可以向锅内滑去喝奶,还不会掉进锅里。

第一只老鼠按照原先计划好了的开始喝牛奶了,另一只老鼠心里却十分不满。

第一只老鼠喝个没完没了,第二只老鼠已经等得不耐烦了,他高喊一声:"够了! 该轮到我了!"他嘴一张,松开了咬在他嘴里的第一只老鼠的尾巴。第一只老鼠掉到了锅里,很快就淹死了。

这时,第二只老鼠高兴地想:"这下可好了,现在他已经淹死了,我就可以独享这一整锅牛奶了。"他开始沿着锅边使劲地爬啊爬,可是怎么也想不出如何能爬上锅去。最后终于饿死了。

---

[1] rim n. 边,缘

[2] descend v. 下降,下来

[3] impatient adj. 不耐烦的,焦躁的

The Smart Hunter
聪明的猎手

The elk[1] is a kind of animals living in the mountains; they were more clever and slimmer than any other animals. The deer-hunters used to lay a giant net as a trap, and then they chased the elks from the other side of the net. When the elks were fleeing in panic[2], they would fall into the net. After many such incidents the elks which survived the hunt finally learned the tricks[3] of those deer-hunters.

Eventually, when the hunters tried to catch them again, the elks rushed backwards, heading towards the hunters instead of running forward. While the hunters were startled, the elks took the opportunity to escape.

After that, the hunters changed their strategy[4]. While chasing the elks, they held the net in their hands instead of laying it on the other side. Unaware of the new hunting method, the elks kept running towards the hunters. They ended up falling headlong into the net and being caught by the hunters.

麋鹿是山林中的一种动物，它们比其他的动物更机灵苗条。在以前，猎人在猎取麋鹿时，总是先布好一张大网，然后从网的另一边追赶麋鹿。麋鹿被追赶得慌张时，就不知不觉撞进网里去了。吃过多次亏以后，侥幸逃脱的麋鹿便识破了这些猎人的诡计。

最终，当猎人再次追赶它们的时候，它们便不再往前跑，而是掉头朝猎人方向冲过来。猎人被冲得惊慌失措，手忙脚乱，而麋鹿就乘机逃掉了。

后来，猎人改变了先前的策略，捕捉麋鹿时，他们不再把网架在另一头，而是手中直接拿着网追赶它们。麋鹿并不知道猎人改变了方法，依然朝猎人方向冲过去，结果正好一头撞进网里去了，被猎人捕获了。

[1] elk n. 麋鹿，驼鹿

[2] panic n. 恐慌，惊慌

[3] trick n. 戏法，把戏

[4] strategy n. 兵法，战略

The Bat who Took Sides[1]

A long time ago, the wild animals in the jungle were always fighting with the birds. After every fierce battle, there were many who were hurt or killed on both sides. The bat did not fight. He only waited to see who won the battle.

At first, the birds beat the wild animals every time, so the bat joined the birds. He flew with the birds to show that he belonged to them.

Then the wild animals won the battle against the birds, so the bat joined the wild animals. He bared his teeth to prove that he was one of the wild animals' group.

In the end, the birds won the battle. The bat again flew back to join the birds. The birds, however, chased[2] the bat away before he said anything.

Then the bat wanted to join the wild animals. However, the lion chased him away, too.

From that time onwards[3], the bat was not accepted by either group. He had to hide in caves during the day. He could only come out at night to look for food when the birds and the wild animals were asleep.

---

[1] take sides 支持一方，袒护   [3] onwards adv. 向上

[2] chase v. 追捕，追赶

没有立场的蝙蝠

很久以前,森林里的野兽经常和鸟类互相争斗。每次激烈的战斗过后,双方都是死的死,伤的伤。蝙蝠从来都不参加争斗,他只是等在一旁观看,看到底最后哪方能获胜。

起初,鸟类每次都能战胜野兽,于是蝙蝠加入了鸟类的行列。他同他们一起飞行,以显示他属于鸟类。

后来,野兽在争斗中击败了鸟类,于是蝙蝠就加入了野兽的行列。还把他的牙齿展示给他们看,以证明他是野兽中的一员。

最后,鸟类在争斗中又击败了野兽。蝙蝠又飞回了鸟类当中。结果还没说话就被鸟类给撵走了。

于是蝙蝠又想加入到野兽的行列中,结果也被狮王赶了出来。

从此以后,蝙蝠既不被鸟类接受也不被野兽接受。他只能白天的时候躲在洞穴里,到了晚上夜深人静鸟类和野兽们都入睡了的时候再出来觅食。

Special Talents[1]

One day, king of the animals, the lion, instructed the monkey to gather all the animals for a parade. The leopard[2], the black bear, the grey wolf, the wild cat, the donkey and the wild hare made up the team.

When the team was lined up and ready, the monkey and lion began the inspection[3]. When the lion reached the end of the line, face to face with the donkey and the wild hare, he started to laugh.

The monkey was surprised and asked the lion, "Your Majesty, what are you laughing at? Is there anything wrong?"

The lion pointed to the donkey and wild hare. "I am laughing at you because you are brainless. How can you include these two small animals into the team? If we were at war, they could not help us to fight!"

The monkey replied, "Your Majesty, you underestimate them. It's true the donkey does not know how to kill, but he is a great trumpeter and he can call the team to keep together. When our team is separated in the mountain or valley, the wild hare can be our messenger because he is a fast runner."

The lion king was impressed with the monkey's remarks. "Yes, I think you are right. I should not ignore that each of them has his own talent!"

[1] talent n. 天赋

[2] leopard n. 豹子

[3] inspection n. 检查,检阅

各有所长

有一天,万兽之王狮王召来了猴子,让他奉命把动物们组织起来操练一支队伍。在这支队伍中,有豹子、黑熊、灰狼、山猫,还有驴子和野兔。

当队伍排成一行,准备好时,狮王和猴子一起前来检阅。当狮王走到队伍的末尾,来到驴子和野兔跟前时,突然哈哈大笑起来。

猴子感到吃惊,便问狮子:"大王,您笑什么? 有什么不妥吗?"

狮子指着驴子和野兔说:"我笑你真是头脑太简单,怎么竟然把这两个小东西也排在队伍里? 要是打起仗来,他们能冲锋陷阵吗?"

猴子回答说:"大王,您低估他们了。的确,驴子不会杀敌,但是他是一个优秀的号兵,他可以帮我们集结队伍。而当我们的队伍分散在高山和深谷的时候,野兔可以帮我们传递消息,他可是短跑健将啊。"

狮子大王被猴子们的一番话说服了,说:"你说得很有道理,他们都各有所长,我不应该忽视他们的专长。"

The New House by the Road

Once upon a time, a man earned a lot of money, so he built a house by the road. As his house was going to be finished, a person walked by and said, "That's too bad. If I were you, I wouldn't build a house like this."

On hearing this, the owner asked, "Then what would you do?"

"I would make every room face the east so that I can see the sunshine when I get up every morning."

The owner thought that was a good idea, so he decided to rebuild[1] the house.

When the rebuilt house was going to be done again, he invited his friend to come to visit his new house.

His friend told him, "You should make every room face the south, so that it will be warm in winter and cool in summer." The man agreed with his friend, so he decided to have the house rebuilt again.

Then, more and more people had different opinions about the house, and they all sounded right. Thus, the man kept rebuilding his house. And the house still wasn't finished after three years.

[1] rebuild v. 重建,改造

马路旁边的新屋

从前，有个人挣了很多钱。于是，他在路边盖了一所房子。当他的房子就要竣工的时候，一个路人经过这里，看见了房子，说道："这个房子盖得可真是不怎么样。如果我是你，我可不会盖这样的房子。"

听到这话，房子的主人赶忙问道："那你会怎样盖它呢？"

"我要让每间房子都朝东，这样每天早上一起来我就能看到太阳了。"

房子的主人觉得这个人的想法很好，于是他决定重新建造他的房子。

就在这个重建的房子马上就要盖好的时候，这个人邀请他的朋友来参观他的新房子。

他的朋友跟他说："你应该让你的房间都朝南，这样才能冬暖夏凉。"这个人觉得他的朋友说得也有道理，于是他决定再次重新建造他的房子。

就这样，越来越多的人都来对房子发表自己不同的见解，而且听起来都很有道理。于是这个人一直不停地在重新建造他的房子，3年以后他的房子还是没有建好。

The Lion and the Elephant

One day, the lion felt very disheartened[1]. He came to the elephant and said, "I think I am not suitable to be the king of beasts anymore. You, with your powerful body and sharp teeth, are not a threatening opponent to me. But when I face a rooster that is much smaller than I, I feel absolutely helpless! When I hear the crow of the rooster, I am so terrified that all my courage vanishes into thin air!"

The elephant lifted his head and looked at the lion with pity. He kept silent for quite a long time and shook his head. The elephant flapped his two big ears vigorously[2] as if he was chasing something off.

The lion was amazed and confused by the elephant's action. He asked the elephant, "Why do you keep flapping your ears?"

The elephant now answered, "Didn't you see a mosquito[3] flying and buzzing beside my ear? I was so afraid that it might fly into my ears—it could be the doomsday[4] for me!"

The lion burst out laughing and said, "This world is full of strange and curious things! I was pouring out my woes to you, saying that I am so afraid of the rooster. But you tell me that you are afraid of the mosquito. See, the rooster is much, much bigger in size compared with the mosquito you are afraid of!"

---

[1] dishearten v. 使沮丧,使失去信心　　[3] mosquito n. 蚊子

[2] vigorously adv. 精力旺盛地,健壮地　　[4] doomsday n. 世界末日

狮子和大象

一天，狮子心情沮丧，他去找大象，说："我觉得自己已经不适合做万兽之王了。虽然你有强壮的身体，锋利的牙齿，却也不是我的对手，可是，当我面对一只比我小很多的公鸡时，我觉得十分无助。我一听见公鸡的啼叫声，就很害怕，以致于所有的勇气都跑到九霄云外了！"

大象抬起头，怜悯地看着狮子，沉默了好久，摇了摇头。他拼命地扇动着两只大耳朵，像在驱赶什么东西似的。

狮子惊奇且困惑地看看大象的动作，问道："你为什么总是不停地扇动着耳朵呢？"

大象这时才开口说："难道你没看到一只蚊子在我耳边飞来飞去嗡嗡地叫个不停吗？我怕它一旦钻进我的耳朵里，我的末日就要来临了。"

狮子听了不禁大笑，说道："这世界真是无奇不有！我向你诉苦，说我怕公鸡，可是你却对我说你怕蚊子。想想看，公鸡好歹要比你所惧怕的蚊子大得多啊！"

The Potter

Once there was a very religious[1] and skillful potter whose pottery was well-known far and wide.

However, he was not satisfied with his finely crafted but fragile pottery. He thought that if the pottery made by him could be unbreakable, his reputation[2] and his business would be even better.

He prayed[3] hard to God to grant his wish for unbreakable pottery.

That night, he dreamd that God said to him, "If you are sure you won't regret it, I will make your wish come true."

The potter said, "Yes, God, I am sure that I will not regret it."

The next morning, the first thing the potter did when he woke up was to test whether God had granted his wish. He went to his workshop, and he used the clay to craft a pot. Then he dried it under the sun. When the pot was dried, he lifted it and dashed it to the floor. The pot did not break! The potter was filled with joy, and the people around were amazed.

The news of the unbreakable pots made by the potter spread very fast. From then on, the potter's business became better, and people from all over the world rushed here for his pottery. He became very rich and famous.

But, the good fortune did not last. After a while, his business slowed down. Although everybody kept praising his products, whoever bought one did not need to buy another because the pots were unbreakable.

As time went by, his economic conditions became bad as the business was worse. Without any methods, he had no choice but prayed to God to grant his wish for his original pottery.

That night, he dreamed that God appeared to him. Tearfully, he begged God to forgive him for his foolishness: "I thought only unbreakable pottery could keep my business going well. However, now I find it difficult to live on."

God said, "Because you admit your mistake, now I will forgive you and make your latest wish come true."

So from then onwards, the potter's original pottery was once again in great demand.

陶工

从前,有一个虔诚信仰宗教而且技艺高超的陶工,他制作陶器的手艺远近闻名。

可是,他为他精心制作的陶器一摔就破而感到不满。他常想:要是我制作的陶器永远摔不破,我的声誉会更高,买卖也会越来越兴隆。

于是,他便向天神祷告,希望能实现他制出的陶器打不破的愿望。

这天夜里,他梦见天神对他说:"如果你将来不后悔,我可以满足你的愿望。"

陶工说:"是的,天神,我决不后悔。"

第二天早晨,陶工起身后做的第一件事就是要看看天神的话是否灵验。他来到工作室,用粘土做了一个罐子,然后把它放在阳光下晾干。罐子晾干后,陶工便举起来使劲往地上摔去,罐子果然完好无损!陶工简直高兴极了,而周围的人都很惊奇。

陶工制作的罐子摔不破的消息,很快传开了。从那时候起,陶工的生意更加兴旺了,人们从世界各地纷纷赶来争购他的陶器,他因此赚了很多钱,而且名气也响当当了。

但是,好景不长。没过多久,生意就清淡下来了。虽然大家对他的陶器赞不绝口,但是所有人买一个就不用再买了,因为他制作的陶器永远摔不破。

生意清淡,日子一长,他的经济情况就变得非常窘迫了。走投无路之下,他只好不断地向天神祷告,希望天神能恢复他原来那样的陶器。

这晚,陶工又梦见天神,他泪汪汪地祈求天神原谅他的愚蠢:"我原以为只有使我的陶器永远摔不破,我的生意才会兴旺。谁知,现在却连生活也没保障了。"

天神说:"你能知道错就好,我原谅你,也满足你最近的愿望。"

从那时起,陶工制作的原来的那种陶器畅销起来了。

---

[1] religious adj. 虔诚的　　　　　[3] pray v. 祈祷,祷告
[2] reputation n. 名誉,声誉

The Fox and the Gadflies[1]

A fox from afar was looking for water to quench[2] his thirst. When he came to a river, he was so thirsty that he did not bother about the swift currents and instantly jumped into the river for a drink. Unfortunately, he was carried to the side of a steep cliff. No matter how he tried, he still could not climb up to the bank because the cliff was very high. Finally, he only clang to the wall of the cliff to keep himself from falling into the water.

A group of gadflies detected the odor of the fox and came rushing to feed on his blood. The fox was painful but helpless to protect himself. Just then, a porcupine[3] came from the mountain to drink water. He pitied the fox being bitten by the gadflies and he cried, "Why do you keep still letting the gadflies bite you and suck[4] your blood? Shall I go down there to help you drive them away?"

The fox said, "Not at all! These gadflies have had themselves filled with my blood. They are now merely playing on my body. If you chase them away, that will attract another group of hungry gadflies to take over their place to suck my blood. That will be even worse!"

---

[1] gadfly n. 牛虻
[2] quench v. 压制，抑制
[3] porcupine n. 刺猬，豪猪
[4] suck v. 吮吸

狐狸和牛虻

一只狐狸由于口渴了,从远处跑来寻找水源。正好看见前面横着一条大河时,他如此地渴,以致于不顾河流湍急,立刻纵身跳了下去要喝水,不幸被激流冲到一个陡峭的石壁边缘。石壁很高,任凭狐狸怎么拼命地挣扎也爬不上来,最后狐狸只好紧紧抓住石壁,不让身子掉入水中。

不久,有一群牛虻闻到狐狸的气味,就蜂拥而至,叮咬他吸他的血。狐狸虽然百般难受,却毫无抵抗的能力。这时候,有一只山里来的刺猬走来也要喝水。他看见狐狸被一群牛虻围攻,觉得他很可怜,就喊道:"你被成群的牛虻叮咬吸血,怎么忍着不动? 我下去帮你将牛虻赶走,如何?"

狐狸回答说:"不必了! 这群牛虻个个都喝饱了我的血,现在只不过是围着我嬉耍而已。如果你把这群牛虻赶跑了,另一群饥饿的牛虻就会飞来取代它们再吸取我的血,那就更糟了!"

The Indecisive[1] Hyena

One day, a hungry hyena was looking for food. He suddenly saw an antelope[2] and a deer were eating on the grass which was not far away. He was very excited, and he approached them cautiously. When he was close enough, he stopped. He could not decide as to whom he should attack first.

By now, both the antelope and deer had seen the hyena and began to run away. The hyena quickly went after them. When they reached a junction[3], the road branched into two. The deer went to the right while the antelope went to the left. When the hyena reached the junction, he stopped and thought, "Which one shall I chase? Go after the deer since he is tall and big. I'm sure to have a delicious and filling meal." The hyena began to chase the deer. Because of his delay, the deer had already run quite a distance.

After a while, the hyena again thought, "No, the deer is big and strong, and runs fast. I'm so hungry; I don't have the energy to keep up with him."

The hyena then turned to the left lane to chase the antelope. Unfortunately, the antelope was already out of sight. When he looked back to the right lane, the deer also disappeared.

---

[1] indecisive adj. 犹豫不决的
[2] antelope n. 羚羊

[3] junction n. 岔路口，联结点

鬣狗狩猎

有一天，一只饥肠辘辘的鬣狗正在找食物吃。忽然，他发现不远处的草丛中，有一只羚羊和一头鹿正在吃草。鬣狗兴奋极了，他悄悄地接近他们。来到猎物前面，鬣狗他决定不了应该先抓哪一只。

就在鬣狗犹豫的瞬间，羚羊和鹿看见鬣狗都逃跑了。鬣狗在后面紧追不舍。忽然，前面出现了岔路，鹿向右边那条路跑去，羚羊向左边那条路逃去。鬣狗在岔道上停了下来，"追哪一只呢？"鬣狗想："追鹿吧！鹿个子大，我定能饱食一顿。"于是，他跑去追鹿。可是，由于刚才的迟疑，他和鹿的距离拉远了。

鬣狗追了几步，又想："不行，鹿身体强壮，跑得又快。而我已经饿极了，根本没有能量追上他。"

于是，鬣狗又向左边岔道的羚羊追去。不幸的是，羚羊已经跑得没影儿了。再回头看看右边岔道，鹿也不见了踪影。

The Grinder[1], the Son and the Donkey

One day, a grinder and his son took their donkey to the marketplace. On the way, they met some laundry[2] women by the river. One of them said, "Look at these two stupid men. They have a donkey to ride on but they would rather walk." The grinder quickly put his son onto the back of the donkey and continued the journey.

Soon, they bumped into a group of old men who were arguing over something. One of them said, "Look, this can well testify my argument. The youngsters nowadays hardly show respect to the seniors[3]. This unfilial child sits comfortably on the donkey and makes his old man walk." The son quickly dismounted[4] and got his father ride on the donkey.

Not far ahead, they saw a mother carrying a baby girl on her back. She said, "This father is so uncaring. How could he have the heart to sit on the donkey and let his little boy walk like that?" At once the grinder asked his son to ride together with him.

The next person they met was a priest who felt very sorry for the donkey. He said, "That poor donkey will get killed by both of you. You might carry it along before it collapses[5]."

The father and son took the priest's advice and alighted from the donkey. They tied its legs together to carry it on their shoulders with a bamboo stick. People on the way crowded round and laughed at them.

When they were about to cross the bridge to enter the town, the donkey could no longer stand being carried upside down. It struggled and fell into the river where it drowned.

The regretful grinder said to his son, "It seems that we can't possibly please everybody. In future, we should perhaps pay less attention to what other people say."

磨工、儿子和驴

有一天，一个磨工带着他的儿子，牵着驴去赶集。路上，他们遇见几个在河边洗衣的妇人，其中一个嚷道："看，这两个笨蛋，放着驴不骑，反而在路上走。"磨工听见了，赶忙将儿子抱到驴背上，自己牵着驴往前走。

不久，他们遇到一群老人正在争论着什么。其中一个老人说："看，这就是对我所说的最好的证明。现在的年轻人，一点都不懂得尊重长辈。你们瞧这不孝的孩子，自己舒舒服服地骑在驴背上，却让他的老父亲走路。"磨工的儿子听了赶忙下来，让父亲骑上驴，他跟在后面走。

走了没多远，遇见了一个背着小女孩的母亲，她看见了说："这个做父亲的真不懂照顾人，怎么可以自己骑在驴背上，却忍心让小孩在地上走呢。"磨工立刻叫儿子上来，一同骑在驴背上。

他们接下来遇见一位牧师。牧师非常同情驴子，说："啊，这个可怜的驴就快被你们给折磨死了。在它昏厥之前，你们最好抬着它。"

父子俩采纳了牧师的建议，跳下驴背，用绳子把驴的腿绑在一起，用一根竹杆子吃力地把驴子扛在肩膀上。一路上惹来众人的围观和嘲笑。

进入城里，驴倒吊着很难受，就挣脱了绳子，扑通一声掉到河里淹死了。

磨工后悔地对儿子说："唉！看来一件事要让每个人都称心是不可能的。以后，我们不必那么理会别人如何说了。"

---

[1] grinder n. 磨工

[2] laundry n. 洗衣店，洗衣服

[3] senior n. 年长者，长辈

[4] dismount v. 从（马背上或自行车上）下来

[5] collapse v. 倒塌，昏倒

No One but Yourself Can Defeat You

A young painter resided in a small narrow house, living on painting portraits[1] before he became famous.

One day, a rich man came by and found the painter paint so meticulously[2] that he liked the paintings and asked him to draw a portrait. They agreed on the remuneration of 10,000 dollars.

After a week, the portrait was done. The rich man came to take the painting as agreed. At this moment, the rich man hit on an evil idea of bullying the unknown young artist, so he refused to pay the remuneration as agreed.

The rich man thought, "The man in the painting is me. If I don't buy this painting, no one will do. Why should I pay so much money for it?" So the rich man said he would only pay 3,000 dollars to buy this painting.

The young artist was stunned, for he had never come across such things. He strongly argued on just grounds, expecting the rich man to abide[3] by the agreement and to be a trustworthy man.

"I can only pay 3,000 dollars to buy the painting. Speak no more." The rich man thought he had won, "I ask you for the last time, will you sell it at 3,000 dollars or not?"

The young artist knew the rich man deliberately went back on his word, so he felt indignant. He said in a firm tone, "No. I would prefer not to sell the painting rather than be humiliated by you. Today you break your word and someday you must pay 20 times."

"What a joke! 20 times will be 200,000 dollars! I won't be stupid to pay 200,000 dollars to buy the painting!"

"Well, we'd better wait and see." the young artist said to the rich man who left angrily.

After the stimulation of such an incident, the painter moved out of this sad place, and followed an acknowledged teacher to work hard night and day. More than a dozen years later, he finally blazed a new way and became popular in the circle of art.

After he left the studio, the rich man had forgotten the artist's painting and words the next day. Until one day, some friends of the rich man simultaneously came to tell him, "Something is so strange! We paid a visit to a famous artist's exhibition of paintings, in which one painting is marked 200,000 dollars and the man in the painting looks exactly the same as you. It is so ridiculous that the title of the painting is Thief."

It came to him as a terrible blow. He immediately thought of what had happened to the painter more than a dozen years ago. If the painting was really the one he broke his promise that year, it would be terrible to him. He went to find the young painter the same night right away. As expected, the painting titled as Thief was no other than that one he had broken his word that year. He quickly apologized to the artist and paid 200,000 dollars to buy the portrait back.

With an undefeated[4] ambition, the young painter made the rich man bend his head.

除了自己,没人能打败你

有一位青年画家,在还没成名前,住在一间狭窄的小房子里,靠画肖像为生。

一天,一个富人经过,看他的画工细致,很喜欢,便请他帮忙画一幅肖像。双方约好酬劳是10000美元。

一个星期后,肖像完成了,这个富人依约前来拿画。这时富人心里起了坏念头,欺他年轻又未成名,不肯按照原先的约定付酬金。

富人心中想着："画中的人是我，这幅画如果我不买，那么没有人会买。我又何必花那么多钱来买呢?"于是富人说只愿花3000美元买这幅画。

青年画家呆住了，他从来没碰过这种事，于是向富人据理力争，希望富人能遵守约定，做个有信用的人。

"我只能花3000美元买这幅画，你别再啰唆了。"富人认为他占据上风。"我问你最后一句，3000美元，卖不卖?"

青年画家知道富人故意赖账，心中愤愤不平。他以坚定的语气说："不卖。我宁可不卖这幅画，也不愿受你的侮辱。今天你失信毁约，将来一定要你付出20倍的代价。"

"笑话，20倍是200000美元耶! 我才不会笨到花200000美元买这幅画。"

"那么，我们等着瞧好了。"青年画家对悻然离去的富人说。

经过这一个事件的刺激后，画家搬离了这个伤心地，随一位名师学艺，日夜苦练。十几年后，他终于闯出了一片天地，在艺术界中，成为一位知名的人物。

那个富人呢? 自从离开画室后，第二天就把画家的画和话淡忘了。直到有一天，富人的好几位朋友不约而同地来告诉他："有一件事好奇怪! 我们去参观一位著名艺术家的画展，其中有一幅画，画中的人物跟你长得一模一样，标示价格200000美元。好笑的是，这幅画的标题竟然是——贼。"

富人好像被人当头打了一棒，他想起了十多年前关于画家的事。如果真的是那个他失信不要的画像的话，那么这件事对自己的伤害太大了。他立刻连夜赶去找青年画家，正如他所料，那幅标题为"贼"的画像正是当年他失信不要的那幅。他赶紧向画家道歉，并且花了200000美元买回了那幅画像。

年轻的画家凭着一股不服输的志气让富人低了头。

---

[1] portrait n. 肖像画

[2] meticulously adv. 仔细地,细致地

[3] abide v. 遵守,坚持

[4] undefeated adj. 不服输的

The Crocodile[1] and the Hyena[2]
鳄鱼和鬣狗

One evening, a hyena met a crocodile on the banks of the Nile River. They stopped and greeted each other.

The hyena said, "How's your life, Mr. Crocodile?"

"Bad, very bad. Sometimes I even cry over some pain and worries. When people see me cry, they always say, 'Those are only crocodile's tears.' This really hurts me. People do not seem to take my feelings seriously."

The hyena said, "My situation is no better than yours. Whenever I stare at those beautiful things of the world, their wonders and miracles[3], I am filled with joy and I break out in laughter as shiny as the morning sun. But the people of the village who see me from afar always say, 'That's only a hyena's laugh'."

一天晚上,一只鬣狗在尼罗河岸边遇到一条鳄鱼,他们停下来,互相致意。

鬣狗说道:"鳄鱼先生,你的日子过得怎么样?"

鳄鱼答道:"不好,很不好,有时候,我因痛苦和烦恼而哭泣。我一哭,人们看见了总是说:'这不过是鳄鱼的眼泪罢了。'这句话太伤我的心了! 人们似乎不重视我的感受。"

鬣狗说:"我的情况比你好不到哪去? 每当我凝视着世界上的美好事物,看到它们的神奇和美妙时,我满心喜悦,不知不觉地就笑了,甚至笑得像朝阳般灿烂。可是,当村庄里的居民远远地看到我时却说:'这只不过是鬣狗的笑罢了。'"

---

[1] crocodile n. 鳄鱼

[2] hyena n. 鬣狗,土狼

[3] miracle n. 不可思议的事,奇迹

The Tortoise and the Scorpion

A Tortoise and a Scorpion had contracted[1] a great intimacy, and bound themselves with such ties of friendship that one could not live without the other.

One day, these inseparable companions, finding themselves obliged to change their habitation, traveled together, but on their meeting with a large and deep river, the Scorpion made a stop, and said to the Tortoise,

"My dear friend, you are well provided for what we see before us, but how shall I get across this water?"

"Never trouble you, my dear friend, for that." replied the Tortoise. "I will carry you upon my back securely[2] from all danger."

On this, the Scorpion, without hesitation[3], got upon the back of the Tortoise, who immediately got into water and began to swim. But he had got halfway across the river, when he heard a terrible rumbling[4] upon his back, which made him ask the Scorpion what he was doing.

"Doing what?" replied the Scorpion. "Well, I am whetting my sting, to see whether I can bore this horny cuirass of yours, that covers your flesh like a shield, from all injuries."

"Oh, ungrateful wretch," cried the Tortoise, "will you, at a time when I am giving you such a demonstration of my friendship, pierce with the venomous sting, the defense that Nature has given me, and take away my life? It is well, however, I have it in my power both to save myself and punish you as you deserve."

So saying, he sunk his back to some depth under water, threw off the Scorpion, and left him to pay with his life for his monstrous ingratitude.

乌龟与蝎子

乌龟和蝎子建立了深厚的友谊,他们相依相伴简直就是形影不离。

一天,这对形影不离的朋友觉得应该改变一下他们的栖息地,于是就决定一起出发。在路上,他们遇到一条又宽又深的河流,蝎子停下来,对乌龟说:

"亲爱的朋友,你能顺利渡过前面这条河,可我怎么过得去呢?"

"不要担心,亲爱的朋友,"乌龟说,"我背着你过河,这样就不会有任何危险了。"

就这样,蝎子毫不犹豫地爬到乌龟的背上,乌龟立即跳入水中朝对岸游去。但是当乌龟游到一半时,他听到背上一阵刺耳的声音,于是就问蝎子在干什么。

"干什么?"蝎子回答道,"哦,我在磨我的刺,看我能否刺穿你那如盾牌般坚固、使你免受伤害的龟壳。"

"哦,忘恩负义的家伙!"乌龟叫道,"我对你这么好,你却企图用毒刺刺穿大自然赐予我的盔甲,想要我的命? 好吧,我有能力拯救自己并让你受到惩罚。"

说着,乌龟将背沉入水中,抛开蝎子,让他为自己的忘恩负义付出生命的代价。

---

[1] contract v. 签订,签契约 [3] hesitation n. 犹豫,踌躇

[2] secure adj. 安全的,可靠的 [4] rumbling n. 隆隆声

The Eagle, the Cat, and the Wild Sow

An Eagle made her nest at the top of a lofty oak; a Cat, having found a convenient hole, moved into the middle of the trunk; a Wild Sow, with her young, took shelter in a hollow at its foot. The Cat cunningly resolved to destroy this chance-made colony. To carry out her design, she climbed to the nest of the Eagle, and said, "Destruction is preparing for you, and for me too, unfortunately. The Wild Sow, whom you see every day digging up the earth, wishes to uproot[1] the oak, so she may on its fall seize our families as food for her young." Having thus frightened, the Eagle was out of her senses, and the Cat crept down to the cave of the Sow, and said, "Your children are in great danger, for as soon as you go out to find food, the Eagle is prepared to pounce upon one of your little pigs." Having instilled these fears into the Sow, she went and pretended to hide herself in the hollow of the tree. When night came, she went forth with silent foot and looked for food for herself and her kittens. But feigning[2] to be afraid, she kept a lookout all through the day. Meanwhile, the Eagle, full of fear of the Sow, sat still on the branches, and the Sow, terrified by the Eagle, did not dare to go out from her cave. And thus they both, along with their families, perished from hunger, and afforded ample provision for the Cat and her kittens.

---

[1] uproot v. 连根拔起,挖倒　　　　[2] feign v. 假装,装作

鹰、猫和野猪

在一棵高大的橡树上，一只鹰在树顶上筑了巢；一只猫找到了一个近便的树洞，住进了树干中部；一头野猪带着她的孩子们在大树底下找到了一个庇护所。狡猾的猫决定破坏这种状况，独占此处。为了实现她的计划，她爬到了鹰巢，说道："真是不幸啊，你正面临着毁灭的危险，我也一样。你看到了，野猪整天在那里刨土，她试图将橡树挖倒，这样就可以抓住我们的家人，作为她孩子的食物了。"这样的威胁使老鹰失去了理智。猫又蹑手蹑脚地爬到野猪的洞穴，说道："你的孩子正面临着极大的危险，只要你一出去找食物，老鹰便准备突袭你的孩子。"向野猪灌输这种威胁后，猫进入到树洞中躲了起来。当夜幕降临时，猫蹑手蹑脚地外出，为自己和孩子们寻找食物，但她装作十分害怕的样子，整天保持警惕。与此同时，老鹰由于十分害怕野猪，就静静地停在树枝上，而野猪由于害怕老鹰而不敢离开自己的洞穴。因此，老鹰和野猪及他们的家人由于饥饿而死亡，而猫和她的孩子们却得到了充足的食物。

The Ass and His Bell

There was a peasant who kept an ass, and all the work this ass did was first-class. His master could not find fit words to sing his praise, fearing in the woods to lose him on a fine day, so he tied on to him a bell that tinkled all the way. The ass was puffed with pride, took on conceited[1] ways. (You understand, he'd heard of decorations.) He quite had come to feel, his life was now the nation's! A mixed delight it is, to join the upper classes (And that may be the same for those who are not asses).

I ought to tell you, till that day, they paid to the ass but scant attention. But till he got his bell, he had no complaints to mention; he'd raided the oats and rye[2], and even the kitchen garden, and when he'd had his fill, went quietly away. But with the bell—I beg your pardon! Our poor distinguished friend! He scarcely had moved a yard, the order round his neck would tinkle hard; next minute, the farmer with his stick, from rye and cabbages had chased him double quickly; another neighbor heard the sound; to warn him off his land, he poked his ribs with just what came to hand. And so our poor celebrity had faded by the fall, till but for skin and bones, and there was no ass at all.

---

[1] conceit n. 自负，自满　　　　　　[2] rye n. 黑麦

驴和他的铃铛

有一个农夫养了一头驴,这头驴把一切事情都做得很不错。连他的主人都觉得找不到合适的词语来夸讲他。一个阳光明媚的日子,主人担心驴会在树林里走失,就给他带了个铃铛,叮叮当当地响了一路。驴骄傲起来了,一副趾高气昂的神情。(要知道,关于勋章,驴也有所耳闻。)他深深感到,自己的生命与国家的命运息息相关。晋升到更高级别,复杂的欣喜之情溢于言表(有些不是驴的家伙或许也会这样)。

我有必要告诉你们,那天之前,其实这头驴并没有引起人们太多的注意。在他没系铃铛时,人们对他并无怨言。燕麦和黑麦他都践踏过,甚至连菜园也糟蹋过,只是他吃饱了,就神不知鬼不觉地溜走了。但是有了铃铛后,实在抱歉得很,我们那小有名气的可怜的朋友啊!他几乎没走几步远,脖子上的勋章便叮叮当当乱响一通。农夫便马上从黑麦和甘蓝地里三步并两步地追了过来,手里还拎着棍子。另一家邻居听到了铃铛声,为了不让驴进自家田地,随手抓起一样东西向他肋骨戳去。所以,到了秋天,我们这位可怜的大名人就垮了,只剩下皮包骨头了,简直都不成样子了。

The Diamond and the Glow-worm
钻石与萤火虫

A diamond happened to fall from the ring of a young lady as she was walking one evening on a terrace[1] in the garden. A glow-worm, who had beheld its sparkle in its descent, as soon as the gloom of night had eclipsed[2] its lustre[3], began to mock and insult it. "Art thou that wondrous thing, that vaunts of thy prodigious brightness? Where now is all thy boasted brilliancy? Alas! In evil hour has fortune thrown thee within the reach of my superior blaze."

"Conceited insect!" replied the diamond, "that owes your feeble glimmer to the darkness that surrounds thee. You know, my lustre bears the test of the day, and even derives its chief advantage from that distinguishing light, which proves thee to be no more than a dark and paltry worm!"

一天晚上，一个年轻女子在花园的平台上散步时，戒指上的钻石忽然脱落了。一只萤火虫看到它坠落那一瞬间的光彩，等它的光芒在夜色中显得暗淡时，就嘲讽、羞辱它。"你不是很了不起吗？你不是吹嘘自己光彩夺目吗？但现在你鼓吹的光芒呢？哎呀！在那不幸的时刻，命运之神将你抛入我这无与伦比的光辉之下了。"

"自以为是的小虫子！"钻石回答，"你微弱的亮光不过是得益于周围的黑暗而已。要知道，我的光芒经得起白昼的考验，并能从白昼的光芒中获得能量，而这光芒却显示你是一只微不足道的小虫！"

---

[1] terrace n. 露台，平台　　　　　　[3] lustre n. 光泽
[2] eclipse v. 使黯然失色

The Lamp[1] and the Sun
灯和太阳

When man learnt how to use the lamp, the lamp felt that it was radiating[2] light, and it became insufferably[3] arrogant at once. "I'm ten times brighter than the sun! People need me the most!"

At this moment, a little gust of breeze blew off the lamp. Then the owner of the house lighted the lamp again with a match, and chided the lamp, "Just behave yourself and emit you properly. And don't boast any more. Even the smallest star in the sky does not need to be re-lighted!"

当人们学会使用油灯的时候,油灯突然觉得自己光芒四射,他顿时摆出了一副傲然自得、不可一世的架势。他说:"我比太阳还要明亮十倍! 人人都离不开我!"

就在这时,一阵微风袭来,把油灯吹灭了。房子的主人划了根火柴重新将油灯点燃,然后语重心长地说:"老老实实发你的光吧,不要再自我吹嘘了。即使是天空中最小的星星,也用不着重新点燃!"

[1] lamp n. 灯   [3] insufferably adv. 不可忍受地
[2] radiate v. 发射(光,热)

The Nails[1] and the Fence

最
寓言 Zui Fable

There once was a little boy with a very bad temper. His father gave him a bag of nails and told him that every time he lost his temper, he should hammer a nail into the fence.

The first day the boy had driven 37 nails into the fence.

Then it gradually dwindled[2] down. He discovered it was much easier to hold his temper than to drive those nails into the fence.

Finally the day came when the boy didn't lose his temper at all. He told his father about it, but the father suggested that the boy now pull out one nail for each day.

The days passed and the young boy was finally able to tell his father that all the nails were gone. The father took his son by the hand and led him to the fence. He said, "You have done well, my son, but look at the holes in the fence. The fence will never be the same. When you are in anger, you leave a scar just like this one. You can put a knife in a man and draw it out. It won't help no matter how many times you say I'm sorry, because the wound is still there. A verbal wound is as bad as a physical one."

---

[1] nail n. 钉子　　　　　[2] dwindle v. 逐渐减少

钉子和篱笆

以前,有个小男孩,脾气很坏,他爸爸就给他一包钉子,让他每次发脾气的时候就往篱笆上钉钉子。

就在第一天,小家伙就已经在篱笆上钉了37个钉子。

慢慢地,他钉得越来越少了,原来他发现控制住自己的脾气要比往篱笆上钉钉子容易得多。

最后,终于有一天,小家伙不再发脾气了。他对爸爸说了这件事,可爸爸却建议他每天再从篱笆上拔出一颗钉子。

日子一天天过去,最后,那个男孩告诉他爸爸钉子都拔完了。爸爸就牵着他的手,带他去篱笆那儿。爸爸说:"儿子,你做得很好。但是,你看看篱笆上的小洞,每根篱笆都绝不会相同的。每次你发脾气的时候,它们就都会像这个一样留下伤疤。你用刀刺伤一个人,可以把刀拔出来。但是,无论你说多少遍对不起都是没用的,因为伤还在那里。言语里的伤害和身体上的伤害同样糟糕。"

第二章

生存之道
The Point of It All

The Fox and the Goat

A fox one day fell into a deep well and could find no means to escape. A goat, came over with thirst, to the same well, seeing the fox, so he inquired if the water was good.

Concealing his sad plight[1] under a merry guise, the fox indulged in a lavish[2] praise of the water, saying it was excellent beyond measure, and encouraging the goat to descend and drink with him.

The goat, mindful only of his thirst, thoughtlessly jumped down, but just as he drank, the fox informed him with the difficulty they were both facing and suggested a scheme[3] for their common escape.

"I have an idea. If," said the fox, "you will place your forefeet upon the wall and bend your head, I will run up on your back and escape, and then help you out afterwards. Then both of us are resured."

The goat readily assented and the fox leaped upon his back. Steadying himself with the goat's horns, he safely reached the mouth of the well and made off as fast as he could.

When the goat upbraided[4] him for breaking his promise, he turned around and cried out, "You foolish old fellow! If you had as many brains in your head as you have hairs in your beard, you would never have gone down before you had inspected the way up, nor have exposed yourself to danger from which you had no means of escape."

---

[1] plight n. 困境
[2] lavish adj. 非常慷慨的
[3] scheme n. 策划，图谋
[4] upbraid v. 责骂，斥责

狐狸和山羊

一只狐狸失足掉到了深井里,不论他如何挣扎仍旧无法爬上去,只好待在那里。一只山羊觉得口渴极了,来到这井边,看见狐狸在井下,便问他井水好不好喝。

狐狸觉得机会来了,心中暗喜,马上镇静下来,极力赞美井水好喝,说这水是天下第一泉,清甜爽口,并劝山羊赶快下来,与他痛饮。

一心只想喝水的山羊信以为真,便不假思索地跳了下去,当他咕咚咕咚痛饮完后,狐狸提醒他他们所共同面临的困境,并且提议说他们可以协力逃出去。

狐狸说:"我倒有一个方法。你用前脚扒在井墙上,再把角竖直了,我从你后背跳上井去,再拉你上来,我们就都得救了。"

山羊同意了他的提议,狐狸跳到他背上,借助山羊的角跳出了井口。狐狸上去以后,赶快独自逃离了。

山羊指责狐狸不信守诺言。狐狸回过头对山羊说:"喂,笨家伙,你的头脑如果像你的胡须那样完美,你就不至于在没看清出口之前就盲目地跳下去,也不会在没有办法逃离的时候将自己置于危险之中。"

The Regretful Deer

One day, a deer was quenching his thirst in the river when he saw his reflection in the water. He started admiring himself. "How wonderful my antlers[1] are! They make me look so handsome!"

The deer turned around and found that his legs were slim and long, and not attractive at all. "Oh, why couldn't my legs be as beautiful as my antlers?" he thought sadly. "My legs are too weak and thin. If I am perfect from the head to the foot, I will be the most beautiful animal. Maybe I could do something to make them look better."

When the deer was deep in his thoughts, a lion came to drink in the river. When he saw the deer, he stopped and crept[2] up slowly. Just as the lion was about to pounce[3] on him, the deer saw the lion. He leapt to the side for safety, and then ran towards the forest as fast as he could.

For some distance it was open ground with hardly any trees. The deer's long legs carried him swiftly across the field. In a short while he was far ahead of the lion. He thought he would be safe among the trees, but he was wrong. As he ran into the forest, his beautiful and branched antlers became tangled[4] in the branches of a tree. He was trapped. The deer pulled and pushed as hard as he could but he could not free his antlers. He could not escape the lion now. In a short while the lion reached the deer. He pounced on the deer and bit him.

"Oh, what a fool I was!" the deer wept as he lay dying. "I hated my long and skinny legs but they were the ones which carried me to safety. Whereas, my beautiful antlers which I was proud of have caused my death."

---

[1] antler n. 鹿角

[2] creep v. 小心翼翼地移动

[3] pounce on 一把抓住

[4] tangle v. 缠绕在一起

鹿的懊悔

一天，一只鹿来到河边喝水。他看到水中自己的倒影，不禁赞叹起来："我头上的鹿角多么的俊秀啊！它们让我看起来那么英俊！"

鹿再转过身子瞧瞧，他觉得自己的腿又细又长，一点儿也不好看。"真可惜，我的腿太瘦长了。"他悲伤地自言自语道，"为何它们不能像鹿角一样完美呢？如果我能从头到脚都完美的话，那我就是动物中最好看的了。唔，或许我可以借助后天的努力来弥补这个缺陷！"

正当鹿沉浸在自己的幻想中时，一只狮子来到了河边喝水。他看见了鹿，于是停下来悄悄靠近鹿。就在他要一把抓住鹿的时候，鹿发现了狮子，赶忙跳向一旁，拔腿向森林跑去。

开始的一段距离是一片没有树木的空地。由于鹿的长腿，不一会儿，他就把狮子远远地甩在了后面，保持一段安全距离。他想如果藏在树林中可能安全，但他想错了。他跑进树林的时候，他那美丽的长角却被树枝缠住了，无法挣脱。他使劲地拉呀，推呀，可他却拔不出他的长角。现在他无法逃开狮子了，很快，狮子追了上来，猛扑向他，咬住了他。

"天啊！我真是愚蠢至极！"鹿临死前懊悔地说道："我轻视助我脱险的这双腿，却以置我死地的角为荣。"

The Bronze Pot and the Clay[1] Pot

It had been raining for a few days. The rivers were flooded and the rubbish in the valley was swept away.

Two pots floating in the rushing current were left helplessly stranded[2] at the river bank, and stopped such terrible travel. They stared at each other. One of the pots was made of glossy bronze while the other was made of clay. The clay pot might look beautiful, but it was not as strong as the bronze one.

The bronze pot told the clay pot, "Come closer, I'm strong enough to protect you! I may have dents[3] here and there but I'm invincible[4]."

However, the clay pot kept going farther and farther, without any intention to approach to him.

"Please don't keep away," pleaded the bronze pot. "I can protect you. I know that clay is more fragile[5] than us. That's why I'm going to take care of you!" The bronze pot moved closer to the clay pot as he was talking.

"No, leave me alone!" said the clay pot anxiously. "It's very kind of you, but please just stay away from me."

"Why?" the bronze pot felt being wronged, "I just want to help you without any other intention!"

"I understand your good intentions. But, as you said, you're unbreakable and I'm fragile. Even if you touch me gently, I'll break into pieces!" said the clay pot.

After the explanation, the bronze pot saw the light.

---

[1] clay n. 粘土

[2] stranded adj. 搁浅的

[3] dent n. 凹痕

[4] invincible adj. 无敌的,不能征服的

[5] fragile adj. 易碎的,虚弱的

铜壶和瓦罐

天空一连下了几天的雨,导致河水泛滥,把山谷一带的垃圾顺流冲走了。

有两个水壶正漂浮于激流之中。他们在无助之下被冲到了岸边,这才停止了可怕的漂浮之旅。两个水壶互相对望。一个用青铜制成的,充满光泽;另一个是用泥土烧成的,虽然设计美观,可是不如前者坚硬。

铜壶对瓦罐说:"快靠到我这里来! 我身躯坚硬,可以保护你呢! 我可能有些缺陷,可是任何东西都无法击破我!"

可是,瓦罐却远远地躲开了,一点儿也没有靠向铜壶的意思。

"别这样!"铜壶说,"我可以保护你。我知道瓦制品比我们脆弱多了,就因为这样,我才要保护你啊!"铜壶边说,边向瓦罐靠了过来。

"不! 别过来!"瓦罐急了,"我知道你的好意,可是让我独处会比较好。"

"为什么?"铜壶觉得很委屈,"我只是想帮助你,可没有别的企图啊!"

"你的善意我很明了。"瓦罐说道,"可是,正如你所言,你是坚硬的铜制品,而我是脆弱的瓦制品。你只要轻轻地碰我一下,我就会粉身碎骨了!"

瓦罐的这一番解释之后,铜壶明白了原因。

The Fox and the Cicada[1]
狐狸和蝉

A Cicada was singing one evening on the branches of a tall tree when a Fox happened to pass by.

"What beautiful singing." said the Fox, peeping[2] up into the branches.

"With a voice like that you must be a very handsome creature. Come down where I can admire your form as well as your voice." But to himself, he said, "Aha, that's Cicada. He'll make me a tasty after-dinner snack[3]."

The Cicada had seen Foxes before. Instead of dropping down himself, he broke off a small leaf and sent it fluttering to the ground. The Fox pounced on it greedily.

"You've given yourself away, Fox." said the Cicada happily, "I've never trusted you since I saw a pile of Cicada wings outside your burrow[4] one day. Now I know I was right about you. You can admire my voice if you like, but I'm not coming any closer to you."

一个傍晚,蝉在一棵大树的枝上引吭高歌,树下恰好有一只狐狸经过。

"这歌声真美妙啊,"狐狸仰望着树枝赞叹道。

"有这样一副好嗓子,我想你一定长得很俊俏,下来吧,那样我不但能欣赏到你的歌喉,还能亲见你的容貌。"可他心里却想:"哦,那可是只蝉,会成为我饭后美味的小点心。"

蝉以前见过狐狸。他没跳下去,只是摘了一小片叶子,扔到地面。狐狸马上贪婪地扑了过去。

"狐狸,你露出真面目了,"蝉高兴地说,"自从在你的洞外看到一堆蝉翼的那天起,我就不再相信你了。现在我知道自己的想法是正确的。若你喜欢我的歌声,那随你便,但我绝对不会接近你。"

[1] cicada n. 蝉

[2] peep v. 窥视,偷看

[3] snack n. 快餐,点心,小吃

[4] burrow n. (兔子等动物挖的)地洞

The Flies and the Honey Pot
苍蝇和蜜罐

There was a potful[1] of honey in the kitchen. The flies lingered[2] over the sweet smell every time they passed by the honey pot. They always dreamed of one day entering the honey pot and enjoying the honey to their hearts' content.

Their dreams came true one day when a butler[3] tipped[4] over the pot and the honey spilt all over the floor. Soon, the sweet smell attracted a swarm of flies. They set their feet in the honey and enjoyed the feast.

When they were stuffed with honey and wanted to leave, their feet were stuck, making them unable to move.

One of the dying flies cried, "How silly we are to sacrifice our lives for short-lived pleasure."

有整整一满罐的蜂蜜放在厨房里。苍蝇们每次飞过蜜罐的时候都会被蜂蜜的香气吸引,在上面久久地徘徊。他们总是梦想着有一天能进到蜜罐里去,将里面的蜂蜜一扫而光。

有一天,他们的梦想终于实现了。一个管家把一整罐的蜂蜜打碎了,蜂蜜流得满地都是。不一会儿,蜂蜜的香气就吸引来了成群结队的苍蝇,他们站在蜂蜜中尽情地享用着。

当他们吃饱了想要离开的时候,忽然发现他们的脚被蜂蜜黏住无法移动了。

临终前,一只苍蝇哭喊道:"我们怎么可以为了一时的快乐而放弃了自己的生命呢!"

[1] potful adj. 一满罐的
[2] linger v. 逗留,徘徊
[3] butler n. 男管家
[4] tip v. 使某物倾斜

The Thief and His Mother

Once, there is a boy living together with his mother. One day, the boy ran hurriedly home from school. His mother noticed his strange behavior and asked him what had happened.

The boy stammered[1], "Mother, this morning my classmate showed me his beautiful writing board. I ... I took it without his knowledge. I know this is not right, but ..."

The mother cut in, "Who said so? After all, he never noticed, did he? Now, this writing board is yours."

"Really?" the boy asked, surprised. "You don't blame me at all?"

"Don't be silly[2]. I won't ever blame you. I'm proud of you, smart boy! Lunch is served, go and eat!"

A couple of days later, the boy brought back a coat and gave it to his mother. The mother tried it on and said, "Hmmm ... this coat suits me perfectly well." She turned around and asked, "Where did you get this?"

"I saw someone hanging their clothes out in the sun," said the boy unashamedly, "I like this one, so I just took it back for you."

"Well done, get me some more next time." His mother gave him a loving hug.

Time passed and the boy grew up to be a thief. He was up to all kinds of robbery at the instigation[3] of his mother. The thief became bolder than ever. One day, he sneaked into a bank and was caught red-handed. As he had committed[4] a serious crime, he was sentenced to death.

The thief was escorted to the execution grounds. His mother followed him, crying her heart out.

Before the execution, the thief requested to have his last words with his mother in private. The woman moved closer to her son to listen attentively. The thief suddenly opened his mouth and bit his mother's ear off!

The mother yelled in pain and scolded[5] her son for being unfilial at that very last moment of his life.

The thief answered scornfully, "If you had scolded me like this when I first stole the writing board, would I have ended up like this?"

小偷和他的母亲

从前,有个孩子和他的母亲相依为命。有一天,孩子慌慌张张地从学校跑回家里。他的妈妈看他这副样子,就问他出了什么事。

孩子结结巴巴地说:"今天我看到同学的写字板很漂亮,就……就趁他不注意的时候,把写字板偷了来。我知道这样做不好,可是……。"

母亲打断了他的话:"谁说这样不好? 反正他又没看见,是吧? 现在写字板就是你的了。"

"真的吗?"孩子吃惊地问道:"你一点儿也不责怪我吗?"

"当然了,我怎么会责怪你呢。我为你骄傲还来不及呢,你真是个聪明的孩子! 午饭已经好了,快去吃饭吧。"

过了几天,孩子带回家来一件外衣,给了他妈妈。他妈妈试了试说道:"嗯,不大不小正合适。"她转头问孩子,"你从哪儿得到的?"

"我看见有人把它挂在外面,"孩子满不在乎地说,"我觉得还不错,就把它拿回来给你了。"

"做得好,下次再多给我拿回点儿别的来。"妈妈给了孩子一个大大的拥抱。

时间如梭,孩子长大,成了一个小偷。在母亲的怂恿下,他养成了偷盗的习惯,到处干坏事,偷东西。小偷的胆子越来越大,这次,他竟然钻进了金库,在作案时被当场抓住。他的罪行太严重了,被判了死刑。

小偷被押赴刑场,他的母亲跟在他身后,哭得伤心欲绝。

临死之前,小偷要求让他和他母亲私下说几句话。母亲走上前,把耳朵凑过去,想听听他有什么要说的,小偷张开嘴,一口把她的耳朵咬了下来!

母亲疼得叫了起来,骂他不孝,犯了罪,临死还要咬掉母亲的耳朵。

小偷冷冷地回答说:"当初我偷写字板的时候,你如果像现在这样痛斥我,我会落到今天这个地步吗!"

---

[1] stammer v. 口吃地说,结结巴巴地说

[2] silly adj. 傻的,愚蠢的

[3] instigation n. 鼓动,煽动,教唆

[4] commit v. 犯(罪)

[5] scold v. 骂,责骂

The Grasshopper and the Ants
蚱蜢和蚂蚁

During the winter, a swarm[1] of ants had a large collection of grain[2] they had dried during summertime. The grain were well kept after the overexposure in the summer.

A starving grasshopper passed by and begged the ants for some food.

The ants asked, "Why didn't you work to store some food during the summer?"

"I was too busy singing during the summer." said the grasshopper, "How could I find spare time?"

The ants replied sternly, "If you kept on singing for the whole summer and forgot about storing food, you can now dance away the winter without eating anything!"

冬天里，一群蚂蚁储存了一大堆他们在夏天收集的粮食。这些经过夏天阳光暴晒后的粮食，都保存得很好。

一只快要饿死的蚱蜢路过那里，看见这群没有断粮之忧的蚂蚁，便向他们祈求食物。

蚂蚁们问他：“你为什么不在夏天储存一些食物呢？”

“我整个夏天都在歌唱，哪还有多余的时间呢？”蚱蜢说。

蚂蚁们便嘲笑他道：“如果你还是整个夏天忙着唱歌，那不如冬天也不要吃东西，整天去跳舞好了！”

---

[1] swarm n. 一大群，云集　　　　[2] grain n. 谷粒

The Poisonous[1] Snake and the Lamb
毒蛇与小羊

Once there was a poisonous snake hiding in some long grass in a field, feeling unhappy with the whole world. When a lamb came to the field to graze[2], the poisonous snake bit him, and then the lamb knew that he fell into danger.

Despite his pain, the lamb asked the snake, "What have I done wrong to make you want to harm me? What have I done wrong to get such a result?"

The snake answered in a hostile[3] manner, "You could have come to attack me. If I didn't protect myself, who knows what you might have done to me. That's why I have to attack you first! So that I can avoid being attacked!" He ate the lamb after finishing his words.

一条毒蛇藏在草堆里,满腹牢骚,感叹世事不公平。一会儿,一只小羊过来吃草。毒蛇便狠狠地咬了他一口,小羊这才知道自己已陷入了险境。

小羊忍着剧痛,质问毒蛇:"我做错了什么,你要这样害我? 我犯了什么罪,要得到这样的报应?"

毒蛇充满敌意地说:"我很肯定,你是来袭击我的。如果我不及时防卫,谁知道你会干出什么坏事来! 所以我要先发制人,置你于死地,这样我才能免于被害啊!"说完便一口把小羊吃掉了。

---

[1] poisonous adj. 有毒的

[2] graze v. 吃草

[3] hostile adj. 不友善的

The Wild Boar[1] Who Sharpenes His Tusks

It was a fine day. The birds were chirping[2] on the branches of the trees. A fox was walking about in the jungle. Suddenly, he heard a strange sound and saw a wild boar sharpening his tusks with a piece of stone.

The fox asked, "Hi, my dear friend, why are you sharpening your tusks? Since it is such a nice day, why aren't you doing something more interesting?"

The wild boar ignored the fox. He continued sharpening his tusks.

最
寓言
Zui Fable

The fox asked again, "I don't see any danger. Everything is calm. There are no hunters, lions or even a bear walking around here. So, why are you busy sharpening your tusks?"

The wild boar now answered, "My dear fox, do you think I sharpen my tusks just for fun? Or because I am bored?"

"So?" said the fox. "I don't see any danger!"

"That is true," answered the wild boar, "but I won't have time to sharpen my tusks when I am really in danger. If I don't get ready now, I will be in a lot of trouble later."

When the fox heard the wild boar's answer, he felt embarrassed[3] and left quickly.

---

[1] boar n. 公猪,野猪　　　　[3] embarrass v. 使窘迫
[2] chirp v. (小鸟)发出唧唧声

野猪磨牙

这天天气晴朗,鸟儿在枝头歌唱,狐狸悠闲地在森林里漫步。突然,传来一阵奇怪的声响,狐狸走过去,看见一只野猪正在用石头磨着他的獠牙。

狐狸问道:"嗨,亲爱的朋友,难得的好天气,你怎么不去干点儿有意思的事情,却在这磨牙啊?"

野猪没有理睬狐狸,继续磨他的牙。

狐狸又说道:"我没有发现任何危险。所有的一切都是那么平静。一个猎人的影子也没有,狮子也不见了,大熊也不在附近徘徊了,你干嘛还要磨牙啊?"

野猪这次回答道:"狐狸老弟,你以为我闲来无事,磨着好玩啊?"

狐狸说:"不是吗?我看不出有什么危险啊。"

"没错,"野猪回答,"可是,当危险来临的时候,我就没有时间磨牙了。现在不做好准备,等遇到麻烦的时候就晚了!"

狐狸听完野猪的回答,羞愧地离开了。

When the Wind Blows

Years ago, a farmer owned a land along the Atlantic seacoast. He constantly advertised for hiring hands. Most people were reluctant[1] to work on farms along the Atlantic. They dreaded the awful storms that raged across the Atlantic, wreaking havoc[2] on the buildings and crops. As the farmer interviewed applicants for the job, he received a steady stream of refusals.

Finally, a short, thin man, well passed middle age, approached the farmer. "Are you a good farmhand?" the farmer asked him.

"Yes, I can sleep when the wind blows. " the little man answered.

Although puzzled by this answer, the farmer, desperate for help, hired him. The little man worked well around the farm, busy from dawn to dusk, and the farmer felt satisfied with the man's work.

Then one night the wind howled loudly in from offshore. Jumping out of bed, the farmer grabbed a lantern and rushed next door to the hired hand's sleeping quarter. He shook the little man and yelled, "Get up! A storm is coming! Tie things down before they are blown away!"

The little man rolled over in bed and said firmly, "No, sir. I have told you, I can sleep when the wind blows."

Enraged[3] by the response, the farmer was tempted to fire him on the spot. Instead, he hurried outside to prepare for the storm. To his amazement, he discovered that all of the haystacks[4] had been covered with tarpaulins[5]. The cows were in the barn, the chickens were in the coops, and the doors were barred. The shutters were tightly secured. Everything was tied down. Nothing could be blown away.

The farmer then understood what his hired hand meant, so he returned to his bed to sleep too, while the wind blew.

当风刮起的时候

几年前，一个农场主在大西洋沿岸拥有一块土地，他经常贴招聘广告雇用人手。可是，很多人都不愿意在大西洋岸边的农场干活，他们害怕大西洋上空狂怒的暴风会破坏房屋和庄稼。所以当这个农场主招工面试的时候，遭到的是一连串坚定的拒绝。

最后，有一个个头不高、略显瘦弱、已过中年的男子来到了农场主面前。"你是个干农活的好手吗？"农场主问道。

"是的，刮风的时候我可以睡觉。"那个矮个子男子答道。

尽管农场主对他的回答有点儿迷惑，可是苦于没有帮手，于是便雇用了他。那个矮个子男子在农场干活很卖力气，从天亮一直忙到天黑，因此农场主对他的工作很是满意。

一天晚上，海面上刮起了咆哮的大风，农场主从床上跳了起来，抓起灯笼就向隔壁雇工住的地方冲去。他晃着那个矮个子男子喊道："快起来！要刮风暴了！快把东西系好，别刮跑了！"

那个矮个子男子在床上翻了个身，坚定地说道："不，先生，我告诉过你，刮风的时候我可以睡觉。"

农场主被他的回答激怒了，气得真想当场把他解雇了。不过，他还是赶紧跑出去为应付风暴做准备。然而，令他惊奇的是，他发现所有的干草垛已经盖好了防水油布，牛在牲口棚里，小鸡在鸡笼子里，门已经闩好，百叶窗也关紧了，一切都拴牢了，什么东西都刮不走了。

此刻农场主才明白雇工的意思，于是，风刮起来的时候，他也回到自己的床上睡觉了。

---

[1] reluctant adj. 不情愿的，勉强的

[2] havoc n. 大范围的破坏，大混乱

[3] enrage v. 激怒（某人）

[4] haystack n. 干草垛

[5] tarpaulin n. 防水帆布

Parable[1] of the Pencil

The pencil maker took the pencil aside, just before putting him into the box.

"There are 5 things you need to know," he told the pencil, "before I send you out into the world. Always remember them and never forget, and you will become the best pencil you can be."

"One: you will be able to do many great things, but only if you allow yourself to be held in someone's hand."

"Two: you will experience a painful sharpening[2] from time to time, but you'll need it to become a better pencil."

"Three: you will be able to correct any mistakes you might make."

"Four: the most important part of you will always be what's inside."

"And five: on every surface you are used, you must leave your mark. No matter what the condition is, you must continue to write."

The pencil understood and promised to remember, and he went into the box with these purposes in its heart.

Now replace the place of the pencil with you. Always remember them and never forget, and you will become the best person you can be.

One: you will be able to do many great things, but only if you allow yourself to be held in God's hand. And allow other human beings to access[3] you.

Two: you will experience a painful sharpening from time to time, by going through various problems in life, but you'll need them to become a stronger person.

Three: you will be able to correct any mistakes you might make.

Four: the most important part of you will always be what's inside.

And five: on every surface you walk through, you must leave your mark. No matter what the situation is, you must continue to do your duties.

Allow this parable of the pencil to encourage you to know that you are a special person and only you can fulfill the purpose to which you were born to accomplish.

铅笔的寓言

铅笔被放入盒子前,铅笔制造商把它拿到一旁。

他告诉铅笔:"在我将你送到世界各地前,你要知道5件事,并时刻铭记在心,永远不要忘记。这样,你才能成为最好的铅笔。"

"第一,你能做出许多伟大的事情。但是前提是,你必须允许别人用手握住你。"

"第二,有时,你会体验被削尖的痛楚,但这种经历会让你变得更优秀。"

"第三,你要能改正自己可能犯下的任何错误。"

"第四,内芯是你身体最重要的部分。"

"第五,你必须在被使用的每一个表面留下你的痕迹。不论在何种情况下,你都得继续写下去。"

铅笔明白了这些道理,并许诺永远铭记。然后,他胸怀这些目标进入了盒子。

现在,换位思考一下,把自己假想成铅笔。永远记住它们,永不忘却,这样你就能成为最出色的人。

第一,你能成就丰功伟业,但是你必须允许上帝对你的掌控,并允许他人接近你。

第二,你会经历生活中的各种艰难险阻,不时体验磨难的痛苦。但是,你需要它们,这样你才能变得更坚强。

第三,你要纠正自己可能犯下的任何错误。

第四,内在品质是你最大的财富。

第五,你必须在你所有路经之地,留下足迹。不论何种情况,你都必须尽职尽责。

让这则铅笔的寓言来激励你,让你知道自己是独一无二的。你与生俱来的目标,只有你自己才能实现。

---

[1] parable n. 寓言,比喻

[2] sharpen v. 削尖

[3] access v. 存取,使用,获得,接近

The Contented Craftsman[1]

There was once a craftsman who was skilled in making cute[2] and pretty clay dolls. These dolls sold well in the market and he earned a good living.

The son of the craftsman grew up having the same talent as his father, and the dolls that he made were sold at the same price as his father's. Nevertheless, his father was not satisfied with it, and kept on finding fault with the dolls he made. After being scolded and criticized by his father, he worked even harder to improve on the quality of the dolls.

Soon the dolls that he made were sold at an even better price than his father's. But the father didn't stop scolding the son; he always criticized his son's dolls. The son's work improved all the time, and now his dolls could sell at five rupees, then at seven or eight, and ten rupees finally!

However, his father never seemed to be satisfied with the dolls he made, and his criticism[3] continued as before.

At last, the son became angry. He said to his father, "Why do you keep criticizing my work? Why don't you admit that my work is far better than yours? Don't you see that what you have made sells only for two rupees while my dolls sell many times more than that? I think that what I have made is now perfect and does not need any improvement!"

Disappointed, the father said, "Son, I understand how you feel. I was the same as you are. That is why my dolls only sell for two rupees each. I am sorry to hear what you have said today, but you will never sell your dolls for more than ten rupees."

"Why?" the son asked.

The father said, "When a craftsman thinks that what he does is perfect, it means there will be no more improvement. When a craftsman is arrogant[4], his skill becomes limited, and the price of his works will remain the same."

骄傲自满的工匠

有一个很会做泥娃娃的手艺人，他做的泥娃娃十分精致漂亮，在市场上销量很不错，他的日子也过得比较富足。

手艺人的儿子长大了，他拥有同他父亲一样的天赋。并且，他做的泥人和父亲做的卖一样的价钱。虽然如此，做父亲的并不满意，总是对他做的泥娃娃挑三拣四。挨了父亲的训斥和批评后，他做起泥人来更加认真了，并且质量也提高了很多。

没多久，他做的泥人售价超越了父亲做的。可是，父亲没有因此而停止责骂儿子。他对儿子做的泥人总是东挑西嫌。儿子更加用心了，做的泥人质量不断提高。现在他做的泥人可以卖五个卢比，不久以后，又提高到七八个卢比，最后提高到十个卢比！

可是，做父亲的仍然不满意，总是在他做的泥人中挑毛病。

儿子生气了，他说："爸爸，你为什么老是挑我的泥人的毛病？为什么你不承认我的泥人比你的好多了呢？你也不看看，你做的泥人至今仍然每个只卖两个卢比，而我的已经超过你好几倍了！我觉得我做的泥人已很完美，不需要再改善了！"

父亲很失望，伤心地说："孩子，我很明白你的心情。当初我就是像你这样，所以到今天我做的泥人每个才卖两个卢比。今天你说这样的话，我很难过，以后你做的泥人的价钱永远不会超出十个卢比了。"

儿子惊奇地问："为什么？"

父亲说："作为一个从事手工业的人，如果认为自己的手艺已到家，没有改进的余地，那么他的技艺也会就此停止。手艺人什么时候自满，他的手艺就从那个时候开始再也不会提升了，手工艺品的价钱也不会提高了。"

---

[1] craftsman n. 工匠（尤指手艺人）　　[3] criticism n. 批评，指责

[2] cute adj. 娇小可爱的　　[4] arrogant adj. 傲慢的，骄傲自大的

The Moon and the Well

One cold night the king called Nasreddin to him and said, "If you're able to spend this night in the courtyard with only your shirt on, I will give you one hundred gold coins[1]!" Nasreddin had no choice but to accept the bet.

In the courtyard Nasreddin stood, quivering with cold. He even felt the messenger of death. But, he saw a stone mill. He began to push it around, faster and faster. When the dawn came, he was sweating[2] all over himself.

The king got up and was surprised to see Nasreddin in high spirits. The king hated to lose one hundred gold coins, so he asked, "Was there the moon last night?"

"Yes."

"Then our bargain[3] is off." said the king, "If there was the moon, it was warm. In that case, even I could have spent the night outside!"

A few months later, the king and his men went hunting. It was hot summer, and at the edge of the desert it was like a furnace[4]. The king and his men were dying of thirst.

They turned toward Nasreddin's house with the hope of getting some water. Nasreddin was sitting on the edge of his well when he heard the voice of the king,"Nasreddin, bring some fresh water! Be quick and serve us!"

"Please make yourself at home." said Nasreddin.

"Where is the water?" cried the king.

"Right here, Your Majesty, you see?" Nasreddin pointed to the well.

"You only show me the water but don't give me a drink!" fumed the king.

"Your Majesty, if the rays[5] of the moon can warm a person, the sight of water can satisfy his thirst."

月亮和水井

在一个寒冷的夜里，国王把纳斯雷丁叫到他的身边说："要是你能只穿一件衬衣在院子里度过这一夜，我就送给你一百枚金币！"纳斯雷丁没有办法拒绝国王，只好接受这个赌注。

纳斯雷丁站在院子里冻得瑟瑟发抖，甚至感受到了死亡的信使。但他看到一盘石磨，便开始推着石磨转，越转越快。当黎明来临时，他已经汗流浃背。

国王起床后，看到纳斯雷丁精神抖擞，大吃一惊。国王不愿意失去一百枚金币，就问："昨晚有月亮吗？"

"有。"

"那我们的赌注无效，"国王说，"要是有月亮，天就很暖和。在那种情况下，就是我也能在外面过夜！"

几个月后，国王和他的随从们去打猎。那是一个炎热的夏天，在沙漠的边缘，天热得像火炉一样。国王和随从们渴得要死。

他们转身向纳斯雷丁家走去，希望弄点儿水喝。纳斯雷丁正坐在井沿上，突然听到国王的声音："纳斯雷丁，端些干净水！快来伺候我们！"

"请不要拘束，自便吧"。纳斯雷丁说。

"水在哪里？"国王叫道。

"陛下，就在这里，你看到了吧？"纳斯雷丁指着井说。

"你只是让我看到了水，却没有让我喝到！"国王发怒说。

"陛下，要是月亮的光线能给人温暖，那看看水也能解渴。"

---

[1] coin n. 硬币

[2] sweat v. 出汗

[3] bargain n. 交易，协议

[4] furnace n. 熔炉，火炉

[5] ray n. 光线，光束

Broken Butterfly Cocoon[1]

Once upon a time in a land far far away, there was a kind old man who loved everything. Animals, spiders, insects...

One day, while walking through the woods, the nice old man found a cocoon of a butterfly. He took it home.

A few days later, a small opening appeared; he sat and watched the butterfly for several hours as it struggled to force its body through that little hole.

Then it seemed to stop making any progress. It appeared as if it had gotten as far as it could and it could go no farther.

Then the man decided to help the butterfly, so he took a pair of scissors[2] and snipped[3] off the remaining bit of the cocoon.

The butterfly then emerged easily.

But it had a swollen body and small, shriveled wings. The man continued to watch the butterfly because he expected that, at any moment, its wings would enlarge and expand to be able to support the body. Nothing happened! In fact, the butterfly would spend the rest of its life crawling around with a swollen body and shriveled wings.

It was never able to fly.

What the man in his kindness and haste did not understand was that the restricting cocoon and the struggle required for the butterfly to get through the tiny opening was nature's way of forcing fluid from the body of the butterfly into its wings so that it would be ready for flight once it achieved its freedom from the cocoon.

Sometimes struggles are exactly what we need in our life. If we were able to go through our life without any obstacles, it would cripple us. We would not be as strong as what we could have been.

And the point is that we could never fly.

破茧的蝴蝶

从前,在一个遥远的国度,有一位心地善良的老人,他喜欢所有的东西,动物啦、蜘蛛啦、昆虫啦……

一天,这位善良的老人在树林里散步的时候,发现了一个蝴蝶茧。他把茧带回了家。

几天后,茧裂开了一个小口。老人坐了几个小时,看蝴蝶挣扎着使劲让自己的身体从小口挤出来。

然后,蝴蝶好像没有什么进展了。似乎它已经到了极限,没法再继续了。

这时,老人决定帮助蝴蝶,他拿了一把剪刀,把茧的剩余部分剪开。

这样,蝴蝶就轻松地出来了。

但是,它的身体肿胀,翅膀又小又皱。老人继续观察蝴蝶,因为他期待蝴蝶的翅膀随时会变大,大到足以支撑它的身体。可是什么也没发生。实际上,这只蝴蝶拖着肿大的身体和萎缩的翅膀爬来爬去,而且它将这样度过余生。

它永远也不能飞了。

在善意和匆忙中,老人不了解,蝴蝶从那个小口破茧而出所需的那种阻碍和挣扎,是大自然用来使蝴蝶的体液挤到翅膀里的方法,这样,一旦蝴蝶破茧而出,就准备好飞翔了。

有时候,挣扎奋斗正是我们生活中所需要的。如果我们可以没有任何障碍地度过一生,我们就会变得软弱。我们就不会变得强壮,而我们本来是可以做到的。

重要的是我们永远都不能飞翔了。

---

[1] cocoon n. 茧

[2] scissors n. 剪刀

[3] snip v. 剪(某物)

Two Snakes Crossing the Road

There was a big snake and a small one living in a pond[1]. It had not been raining for a long time, and the pond was nearly dried up. The snakes decided to move away.

The small snake told the big one, "If you go first and I follow you, people will see us as ordinary[2] snakes passing by. I bet they will beat us to death."

The big snake looked at the small one and asked, "So, have you any smart idea to save us from death?"

"I suggest we hold our mouths together and you carry me on your back. This way, people will surely regard us as holy spirits[3]." answered the small snake.

The big snake had no objection[4] to that, so he carried the small snake on his back and they started to cross the road, holding their mouths together. When people saw them coming, they kept at a distance and said, "Those are holy spirits, we'd better stay away!"

Hence, both snakes survived.

---

[1] pond n. 池塘，水塘

[2] ordinary adj. 普通的，平常的

[3] spirit n. 精神，灵魂

[4] objection n. 反对

两蛇过路

在一个池塘里，住着两条蛇：一条大蛇和一条小蛇。老天久旱无雨，池塘里的水都快干了，于是，大小两条蛇决定搬迁。

小蛇对大蛇说："如果你在前面走，我在后面跟着，人们就会认为我们是路过的普通蛇，这样必定会把我们都打个稀烂。"

大蛇看了小蛇一眼，问道："那你有什么妙计，可免我们一死？"

小蛇回答说："不如我们用嘴互相衔着，你背着我走。人们见了，一定会认为我们是神灵。"

大蛇没有异议，于是他们便用嘴互相衔着，大蛇背着小蛇越过大路。人们见了都赶紧回避，并且说："这是神灵，快闪开！"

于是，大小两蛇保住了性命。

最 寓言
Zui Fable

Carrots, Eggs, Coffee and Boiling Water

A daughter complained to her father about her life and how things were so hard for her. She did not know how she was going to make it and wanted to give up. She was tired of fighting and struggling. It seemed as if one problem was solved, and a new one arose.

Her father, a cook, took her to the kitchen. He filled three pots with water and placed each on a high fire. Soon the pots came to a boil. In one he placed carrots, in the second he placed eggs, and in the last he placed ground coffee beans. He let them sit and boil, without saying a word.

The daughter impatiently waited, wondering what he was doing. In about twenty minutes he turned off the burners[1]. He fished the carrots out and placed them in a bowl. He pulled the eggs out and placed them in a bowl. Then he ladled the coffee out and placed it in a mug[2]. Turning to her, he asked: "Darling, what do you see?"

"Carrots, eggs and coffee." she replied.

He brought her closer and asked her to feel the carrots. She did and noted that they were soft. He then asked her to take an egg and break it. After pulling off the shell[3], she observed the hard-boiled egg. Finally, he asked her to sip the coffee. She smiled, as she tasted its rich aroma.

"What dose it mean, father?" She humbly asked.

He explained that each of them had faced the same adversity—boiling water, but each reacted differently. The carrot went in strong, hard, and unrelenting. But after being subjected to the boiling water, it softened and became weak. The egg had been fragile and its thin outer shell had protected its liquid interior. But after sitting through the boiling water, its inside became hardened. The ground coffee beans were unique, however. After they were in the boiling water, they had changed the water.

胡萝卜、鸡蛋、咖啡和沸水

女儿向父亲抱怨她的生活,觉得事事艰难。她不知如何应对,想要放弃。她厌倦了不断的抗争和奋斗,好像刚解决一个问题,另一个问题就出现了。

她的父亲是位厨师,把她带进了厨房,分别在三个锅里灌上水,然后放到火上烧。很快,水开了。他把一些胡萝卜放入第一个锅里,把几个鸡蛋放入第二个壶里,把磨好的咖啡豆放入第三个锅里,并将锅放好等着沸腾,一言不发。

女儿很不耐烦地等着,对父亲的所作所为百思不得其解。大约二十分钟以后,父亲关上炉火,把胡萝卜倒进一个碗里,又把鸡蛋倒进一个碗里,将咖啡盛倒一个大杯子里,然后转过身,对她说:"亲爱的,你看见什么了?"

"胡萝卜、鸡蛋和咖啡。"她回答。

父亲让她靠近点去摸胡萝卜,她摸了摸,觉得胡萝卜变软了。然后,他让她拿个鸡蛋,敲破。把蛋壳剥掉后,她发现鸡蛋熟了,硬了。最后,父亲让她尝尝咖啡,她尝了一口,香气四溢,不禁笑了。

"父亲,这是什么意思啊?"她谦虚地问道。

父亲解释说,这三样东西面临同样的困难——沸水,但它们的反应却迥然不同。胡萝卜原本强硬、不屈不弯,可是经沸水煮后就变软弱了。鸡蛋原本脆弱,薄薄的蛋壳保护着里面的蛋液。但经沸水一煮,蛋液就变硬了。不过,最具特色的还是磨碎的咖啡豆,一放到沸水中,它们竟然把水改变了。

---

[1] burner n. 炉子

[2] mug n. 圆筒形有柄大杯

[3] shell n. 蛋壳,贝壳

The Beggar and the Miser[1]

One day, an old beggar went to the village. He knocked at the door of a rich man to beg for food. This was a big house and at the side was a granary[2] built with a big padlock. The owner of the house was a miser although he was rich and known for never helping anyone.

The beggar was aware of his reputation but still pleaded, "Will you give me a bit of butter or milk?"

The miser said impatiently[3], "No! Go away at once!"

"Perhaps you can sweep out for me a bit of grain or beans." The hungry beggar had to continue to beg before that bad man because he was too hungry.

"There isn't anything in my house!" the miser refused.

"How about a little bit of bread?" the beggar insisted, "Only a mouthful of food and I will be very grateful."

"Go away! I don't have bread!"

"How about some water? I am very thirsty."

"I don't have water."

The beggar then said sadly to him, "My friend, why are you here? You should go to some kind-hearted folk[4] to beg for food because you are poorer than anybody else."

---

[1] miser n. 吝啬鬼，守财奴

[2] granary n. 谷仓，粮库

[3] impatiently adv. 急躁地，无耐心地

[4] folk n. 人们

乞丐和吝啬鬼

从前有一个老乞丐,有一天,他来到村庄里,他敲了一个有钱人家的门,想要点儿东西吃。这是一座很大的房子,旁边有一个很大的粮仓,门上挂着一个大铁锁。这户人家的主人是个吝啬鬼,他很有钱,但是出了名的从来不肯帮助别人。

乞丐也知道他吝啬,但还是央求他:"您能不能给我一点儿牛油或者牛奶?"

吝啬鬼不耐烦地回答:"不行!你快给我滚开!"

"说不定,您家里还能扫出一把谷子或者豆子吧?"乞丐实在是太饿了,他不得不在这个心肠很坏的人面前继续哀求。

"我家里什么也没有!"吝啬鬼一口回绝了他。

"那就请您给我一点儿面包吧,"乞丐说,"只要给我一点点儿吃的,我一定会感谢您的。"

"去你的吧,我没有面包!"

"那就给我一口水喝吧,我口渴了!"

"我没有水!"

乞丐伤心地对他说:"我的朋友,那你还待在这里干什么?你快去找那些善良的人讨些饭吃吧,因为你比谁都穷啊!"

The Lion and the Apple Tree
狮子和苹果树

Once upon a time there was a bear, a deer, and a rabbit. These animals were very hungry. In the middle of a beautiful meadow[1] there was a big, juicy[2], sweet apple tree. But there were two reasons why the animals could not get the juicy apples. One reason was that the apples were too high. Another reason why they couldn't get the apples was that there was a swift and sly lion guarding the tree.

One day, the deer ran in the meadow and said, "Run! Run! Hurricane[3] is coming!" The lion asked in fear, "What should I do?" The deer said, "For God's sake, run!" So when the lion was gone the animals went to the tree and tried to pile up the animals from biggest to smallest to reach the apples. That didn't work, so they ran around the tree until they were dizzy and then hit the tree. Suddenly, the apples came down! And they lived "appley" and dizzily after.

从前,有一只熊,一只鹿和一只兔子,这些小动物们都非常饿。在草地的中间长着一棵苹果树,上边的苹果又大又甜,汁又多。但是有两个原因使这些小动物们够不着这些多汁的苹果,一个是因为这些苹果长得太高了,另一个是因为有一只反应敏捷且狡猾的狮子在看着这棵苹果树。

一天,小鹿跑到草地上说:"赶紧跑! 赶紧跑! 飓风就要来了!"狮子惊慌地问:"那我该怎么办啊?"小鹿说:"看在上帝的份上,赶紧跑啊!"于是狮子就跑了。小动物们都来到苹果树下,大家从大到小一个压着一个叠在一块准备摘苹果,但是没摘到,这时他们就开始围着苹果树一直跑,直到他们跑晕了撞到了苹果树,这时,苹果突然掉下来了! 之后它们就晕晕地在苹果堆里享受起来了。

[1] meadow n.草地
[2] juicy adj.多汁(液)的
[3] hurricane n.飓风

The Monkey That Wanted to Swim
猴子游泳

A monkey was playing at the riverbank when he saw some fish swimming freely in the water. He admired them and thought, "The fish are so happy!"

After a while, a flock of ducks came by and swam in the river. They had great fun in the water.

The monkey stared at them and he thought to himself, "Swimming is fun and not difficult to learn. Why don't I go into the water and try? I'm sure that even without any practice[1], I'll be able to swim!" He jumped into the water without hesitation[2].

When he was in the water, he realized that swimming was not so easy as he thought. He struggled with all his might to get out of the water but in vain. Finally he drowned[3].

一只猴子跑到河边玩耍,看见河里的鱼儿游来游去,轻松自在,真是羡慕不已,便想:"鱼儿是多么幸福啊!"

不一会儿,一群鸭子游过。它们在水里玩得很开心。

猴子看得出神,暗想:"看来,游泳这玩意儿又好玩又不难学,我不妨下水试试! 我敢肯定,不用练习,我也能游!"说着,毫不犹豫地一头跳进了水里。

猴子跳入水里后,才知道游泳不是他想象中的那么容易。他拼命地在水里挣扎想出来,但徒劳无用,后来就淹死在河里了。

---

[1] practice n. 练习

[2] hesitation n. 犹豫

[3] drown v. 淹死,溺死

The Wolf and the Shepherd[1]

There was once a shepherd who looked after his flock of sheep in a meadow every day. One day, he saw a wolf stopping at the edge of the meadow and staring at the sheep. The shepherd was very worried. He held on to his staff as he watched the wolf.

However, the wolf did not try to chase after any of his sheep. Day after day, he came and rested on the ground. The shepherd got used to seeing the wolf there. He became less worried about the wolf.

One day the wolf even followed him as he took his flock to another meadow. Feeling now that the wolf was quite harmless, he said to the wolf, "Why do you come here every day? You don't seem to have interest in the sheep at all."

The wolf said, "You don't have to worry about me. I don't even eat meat any more. I'm a vegetarian[2] now, and I feel healthier."

"Is that true?" Asked the shepherd, surprised.

"You have seen it for yourself. Otherwise, how could I come here every day and not attack your sheep?" The shepherd nodded his head, and the wolf continued, "In fact, you can safely let me take care of your sheep for you when you are not around."

The shepherd was not sure of that. But in the following days, the wolf kept coming to sit among the sheep and the shepherd grew to trust him.

One day, when the shepherd had to go to the town to buy something, he said to the wolf, "Please help me to look after the sheep while I'm away. I trust that you will not harm any of them."

"Of course you can trust me," said the wolf. "I'll take good care of them."

As soon as the shepherd was at a safe distance, the wolf pounced on the sheep. When the shepherd returned, he found most of his flock dead and a few sheep huddled together, shivering and bleating in fear. Shocked and angry, he shouted at the wolf, "How could you do this to me? I thought you were my friend!"

The wolf laughed as he ran off, saying, "You stupid shepherd, when have a wolf and a shepherd ever been friends?"

狼和牧羊人

从前，有个牧羊人，每天都在草地照看着他的羊群吃草。一天，他发现一只狼站在草地边上盯着他的羊群。牧羊人心里很担忧。他手里紧紧地握着牧羊鞭，眼睛紧盯着狼。

然而，狼却没有侵犯羊群的意思。日复一日，狼每天都来到草地上，但只是静静地站在那里。牧羊人习惯了狼的到来，开始放松警惕。

一天，当牧羊人把羊赶到另一片草地的时候，狼又跟来了。牧羊人现在觉得狼确实没有什么恶意，于是跟狼说："你为什么每天都来这？你似乎对羊群不感兴趣？"

狼说："你不用害怕我，我已经不吃肉了，我现在是一个素食主义者，而且我还觉得比以前健康了。"

"真的吗？"牧羊人惊讶地问。

"正如你亲眼所见，不然我怎么可能每天来到这里而没有袭击你的羊呢？"牧羊人点了点头，狼又接着说道："实际上，当你不在的时候，你可以放心地把羊群交给我。"

牧羊人对此还是不太放心。但是接下来的几天里，狼每天都坐在羊群中间，渐渐地，牧羊人开始相信他了。

一天，牧羊人不得不去镇上买点东西，他对狼说："我不在的时候，请你帮我照看羊群吧，我相信你不会伤害它们中任何一个的。"

"你当然可以相信我，"狼说，"我会好好照看你的羊的。"

当牧羊人刚一走出狼的视线，狼就向羊群扑了过去。牧羊人回来以后，发现大部分的羊已被狼吃掉，剩下的都缩成一团，因为恐惧而颤抖和哭泣。牧羊人非常生气地冲狼大喊："你怎么可以这样对我，我把你当作我的朋友啊！"

狼笑着跑开了，说道："愚蠢的牧羊人，你什么时候见过把牧羊人当作朋友的狼？"

---

[1] shepherd n. 牧羊人　　　　　　　[2] vegetarian n. 素食者，食草动物

Two Lazy Men

Once upon a time, there lived a very lazy man. He was so lazy that he avoided doing anything. He had no money to settle[1] his rent[2] and the landlord kindly packed some cookies for him before asking him to leave.

"Where shall I go?" the lazy man asked himself. He hung the packet of cookies around his neck and began to wander about. He walked and walked until he was hungry.

"Oh, I am hungry and I should have some cookies now, but it is too troublesome to unpack them." He was too lazy to unpack the packet, so he remained hungry as he continued his journey.

"How is it that no one is around?" he thought while walking, "How nice if I could meet someone and ask him to unpack the packet for me."

Then the lazy man met a man in a hat who had his mouth widely open.

He asked, "Why do you open your mouth so wide? Are you very hungry? Why don't you help me unpack my packet around my neck? There are some cookies. Then we can eat together."

The man replied, "My brother, what do you expect of me? My hat scarf[3] has loosened and I find it troublesome to fasten[4] it. I just leave my mouth open so that the lower jaw can tighten it."

[1] settle v. 平息，解决

[2] rent n. 房租

[3] scarf n. 围巾，头巾

[4] fasten v. 系牢，关紧

两个懒汉

从前，某个地方住着一个非常懒惰的人。因为这个人懒得什么也不肯干，所以没钱交房租，后来被房东赶了出去。房东还好心地给了他几块饼干，放进一个包裹里。

"我该去哪儿呢?"懒汉问自己，他把装有饼干的包裹挂在脖子上，毫无目标地在路上走着。懒汉走着走着，肚子不知不觉饿了起来。

"哎，肚子饿了，真想吃饼干，可是要打开包裹，真是太麻烦了!"这个懒汉因为懒得动手打开包裹，所以宁愿忍着饥饿继续前行。

他边走边想:"一路上怎么没碰见人呀? 要是有人就好了，我可以请他帮忙打开包裹。"

这时，这个懒汉遇到了一个戴着帽子、张着大嘴巴的男人。

懒汉问道:"这位先生，你一定是饿极了，才把嘴张得那样大吧? 不如你来替我解下挂在脖子上的包裹，里面有一些饼干，咱们一块吃怎么样?"

那男人回答:"你说什么呀，我的老弟，我帽子的绳子松了，而系起来又是那样的麻烦，所以才张着嘴巴，好让下巴去绷紧绳带啊!"

The Proud Rooster

In a small village there lived an old woman who reared[1] a large brood[2] of chickens. Among them was a strong and handsome rooster.

The old woman loved the rooster very much, as if he were her own child.

He therefore commanded a lot of respect, and it made him proud and arrogant.

One day, a cat was sunning himself when the rooster came by and said, "Get lost! I want to look for food here. Don't stand in my way."

"I'm only sunbathing here for a while. Can't you go to another place to look for food?" the cat said.

The rooster felt that the cat was being disrespectful. He angrily jumped onto the cat and pecked him repeatedly. In terrible pain, the cat was about to bite off the rooster's neck when the old woman suddenly appeared. She chased the cat away with a stick.

Seeing that, the rooster became even more arrogant. "Everyone should acknowledge my special position in this place," the rooster proudly declared.

One night, when the hens were resting in their coop[3], they talked about the rooster. "Only the rooster can make everyone scared. He's really terrific. We must make him our king," said a hen.

"Wait a minute," said a brown hen. "In the jungle there is an animal that is stronger than the rooster. It is the fox. If the rooster can defeat him, we'll make him the king."

The other hens agreed and told the rooster about it.

"I'll defeat the fox." said the rooster confidently.

The next morning, the rooster and the hens went to the jungle to look for the fox. When they reached the edge of the jungle, none of the hens were brave enough to go farther. They were afraid the fox might suddenly appear.

The arrogant rooster bravely carried on. He soon met the fox and at once flew at him. Using his sharp spurs, he scratched the fox. The fox caught hold of the rooster in a tight grip. He very easily broke the rooster's neck and feasted on him.

骄傲的公鸡

在一个小村子里,有一个老妇人喂养了一群小鸡崽,在这群小鸡崽中有一只强壮、潇洒的公鸡。

老妇人非常喜爱这只漂亮的公鸡,爱他如同自己的孩子一般。

因此,这只公鸡受到很多礼遇,于是处处摆出一副不可一世的姿态。

有一天,猫在院子里晒太阳。公鸡骄傲地走过去,喝斥道:"滚开,我在找食物,别挡着我的去路。"

"我只是在这儿晒会儿太阳,你要找食物为什么不到别处去?"猫说。

公鸡感到猫竟然对他不敬,顿时勃然大怒,他跳过去,用嘴不停地狠狠地啄猫。忍受不了疼痛,猫想扑过去咬公鸡的脖子,老妇人突然跑过来,用棍子把猫轰跑了。

看到这幅情景,公鸡变得更加骄傲了。"所有人都必须承认我在这个家里的特殊地位,"公鸡骄傲地宣布。

一天晚上,一群母鸡聚在鸡舍里休息。大家谈论起这只公鸡。有只母鸡说:"公鸡大哥使每个人生畏,真是太了不起了! 我们应当推举他为王。"

"等一等!"一只棕色的母鸡说,"丛林中有一个动物比这只公鸡强大,那就是狐狸,如果公鸡能战胜狐狸,我们就选他为王。"

群鸡同意了这个方案并把这件事情告诉了公鸡。

"我一定要打败狐狸。"公鸡得意忘形地说道。

第二天一早,母鸡们带领着公鸡到密林里去找狐狸,当她们到达密林边时,没有一只母鸡敢往前再迈一步,她们害怕狐狸会突然出现。

而那只被傲气冲昏了头的公鸡却趾高气扬地向密林深处走去。公鸡一见狐狸,便狂妄地扑过去,用他锋利的爪子刮伤了狐狸。但狐狸紧紧地抓住公鸡,轻易地咬断了公鸡的脖子,吃了一顿丰盛的早餐。

101

最
寓言
Zui Fable

---

[1] rear v. 饲养,喂养   [3] coop n. 养鸡的笼子

[2] brood n. 一窝雏鸟

Mother Crocodile and the Wolf

Long ago, there lived a wolf in the dense jungle. In the same jungle, in a river, lived a crocodile with her six babies.

The mother crocodile wanted her children to grow up strong and intelligent. She needed a good teacher for her children. She had heard that the wolf was a well-known teacher, so she went to see him about this.

"I'm always busy during the daytime," the wolf said. "I can only teach your children if they stay here with me." The mother readily agreed to the arrangement. The next day, she sent all her six children to the wolf's home.

At the sight of the fat and healthy young crocodiles, the wolf had to control his urge to grab them. He greeted them warmly and the mother crocodile returned home.

The young crocodiles sat in front of the wolf as he started to teach them to read. They obediently did whatever their teacher asked them to do. Later, the wolf asked them to read on their own.

While they were reading, the wolf pretended to fall asleep. Actually, he was watching the six young crocodiles and thinking of a way to get them for food! On seeing that their teacher had fallen asleep, the young crocodiles started leaving the house to play outside. As the last one was trying to slip out, the wolf caught him and ate him.

The next day, the mother crocodile went to the wolf's house to visit her children. The wolf brought out the fifth child twice so that the mother crocodile would think all her children were safe. Satisfied, the mother crocodile returned home.

After that, the wolf ate up another of the young crocodiles. "How good life is this." he thought to himself. "Each day I have a young crocodile to eat!"

On the third day, the mother crocodile once again came to see her children. The wolf repeated what he had done before. He brought out the fourth child three times. After she had left, the wolf ate another of her children. Only three young ones were left.

On the fourth day, the mother crocodile came again. The wolf brought out each of the rest three young crocodiles twice. When the mother crocodile had counted her six children, she returned home happily.

The wolf then ate another of the young crocodiles. He repeated it day after day till he had eaten up all the young crocodiles. Then he disappeared into the jungle.

On the seventh day, the mother crocodile once again went to the wolf's home. She found it empty. Sadly, she realized what had actually happened.

"I only knew that the wolf was clever, but I did not realize his real nature." she said regretfully to herself.

鳄鱼妈妈和狼

从前,在丛林的深处住着一只狼。在同一片丛林中的一条小河里,住着鳄鱼妈妈和她的六个孩子。

鳄鱼妈妈想让自己的孩子既聪明又长得强壮,她想找一个好老师来教她的孩子们。她听说狼是个很有名的老师,于是就去找狼,想让他来教教她的孩子们。

"白天我都很忙,"狼说,"如果让我来教你的孩子们,你就必须把他们放在我家里。"鳄鱼妈妈欣然同意了狼的安排。第二天,她把她的六个孩子都送到了狼的家里。

狼看见六只肥肥胖胖的小鳄鱼时,极力控制他想抓住他们的欲望。他热情地欢迎小鳄鱼们的到来,然后,鳄鱼妈妈回家了。

小鳄鱼们坐在狼面前跟他一起读书。老师怎样说,他们就怎样做。一会儿,狼老师就开始让小鳄鱼们自学了。

当小鳄鱼们自学的时候,狼假装在一旁睡着了。实际上,他一直盯着这六只小鳄鱼,思考着怎样才能把他们变成自己的盘中餐。看见老师睡着了,小鳄鱼们就跑到外面玩去了。当最后一只小鳄鱼正想往外溜的时候,狼一把抓住了他,把他吞到了自己的肚子里。

第二天,鳄鱼妈妈来到狼的家中看望她的孩子们。狼把第五只小鳄鱼抱出来了两次,鳄鱼妈妈看到自己孩子们都安然无恙,于是就心满意足地回家去了。

就这样,狼又吃掉了一只小鳄鱼。"生活是多么的美好啊,"狼暗自想,"每天都有一只新鲜的小鳄鱼吃!"

第三天,鳄鱼妈妈又来看望自己的孩子,狼又如法炮制地把第四只鳄鱼抱出来了三次。当鳄鱼妈妈走后,狼又吃掉了一只小鳄鱼,这次只剩下三只小鳄鱼了。

第四天,鳄鱼妈妈又来看望自己的孩子。狼把剩下的三只小鳄鱼每只都抱出来了两次。鳄鱼妈妈数了数自己的孩子,高兴地回家去了。

于是,狼又吃掉了一只小鳄鱼。他就这样日复一日地吃光了所有的小鳄鱼,之后就消失在森林里了。

第七天,鳄鱼妈妈又来狼的家看望自己的孩子,她发现屋子空了。她终于意识到发生了什么。

"我只想到了狼很聪明,却忽视了他的本性。"鳄鱼妈妈后悔不已。

The Lark's[1] House-moving

Long, long ago, two birds and their fledglings[2] lived near a farm. Every morning and evening, the parents would go out to find food for their little ones. One day, when they brought the food home, the baby birds said to them frantically, "Pa! Ma! This is the end of us!" Startled, the parent birds asked, "What happened? Tell us quickly."

The baby birds said, "We heard that the owner of the farm has asked his relatives and friends to come and help harvest the crops tomorrow. We will have nothing left to eat." Their parents comforted them, saying, "Don't worry about it. No matter what it is, his relatives and friends will definitely not come." The baby birds were confused, but they believed there must be some truth in their parents' words, because they were older, more experienced, and must know more. Reassured, the baby birds ate heartily. Several days went by, and true enough, none of the farmer's relatives and friends came to help with the harvest.

Then, a few more days later, when the parent birds came back with food, their little ones told them again, "This is the end! We heard that the farmer has asked all his children to come home tomorrow to help reap the crops. We will have no more food. We are in serious trouble!" Their parents laughed and reassured them, "No! It won't happen! Don't worry. Their children will definitely not come to help them. Don't be afraid." The baby birds were happy to hear that. Their parents had made the correct prediction[3] last time, so they must be right this time. The family enjoyed their dinner joyously, and truly, as predicted, none of the children came back to help the farmer harvest his crops.

Again, several days went by, and when the parent birds returned to the nest with dinner for their babies, the little ones again told them, "We are in trouble! We are in danger! We heard that the farmer and his wife have decided to harvest the crops by themselves tomorrow. They are not going to rely on others or ask for help." This time, the parents were really worried and said, "This is indeed the end!" The little ones asked, "This is strange! Why is that? The last two times we told you that they were going to get help from their relatives, friends, and children, you were delighted and said that nothing would happen. Why are you so shocked this time that they are going to reap the harvest by themselves and not rely on others?" The parents explained, "You don't understand. If they really rely on themselves, they will definitely[4] do it. You cannot depend on others. Now that they have decided to be self-reliant, they will definitely do it. We will have no more food. We would better move to another farm."

百灵鸟搬家

很久以前,有两只鸟跟它们的孩子一起住在一个农场旁边。每天早晚,它们会出去找食物回来给孩子们吃。有一天,当它们带食物回去的时候,那些小鸟很激动地跟它们说:"爸爸、妈妈,完了!完了!"它们两个就很惊奇地问:"有什么事?赶紧跟我们讲。"

那些小鸟说:"听说明天农场主人会去找他的亲戚朋友来帮他收割,那我们就没东西吃了。"它们的父母安慰它们说:"别担心,不管怎么样,他的亲戚朋友一定不会来帮忙的。"那些小鸟感到很困惑,不过父母讲的话一定有它们的道理,因为它们年长,经验丰富,一定知道得更多。所以它们就安心了,吃得很开兴。几天以后,果然农场主人的亲戚朋友都没有来帮忙收割。

过了几天,当小鸟父母带食物回来时,它们的小孩又说:"完了!完了!听说那个农民已经叫他所有的小孩明天回来帮他收割,那我们就没东西吃了,麻烦大了!"那对小鸟父母笑嘻嘻地说:"不会!不会!你们放心,他们的小孩一定不会回来帮他们忙的,你们不要怕。"小鸟听了很兴奋,上次它们的父母讲对了,这次一定也对,大家就很开心地吃晚餐。果然如此,没有一个孩子回来帮农民收割。

又过了好几天,有一次小鸟父母从外面带晚餐回来给它们的孩子吃的时候,那些小鸟又说:"麻烦了!危险了!听说农场主人夫妇决定明天要自己收割了,他们不靠外人,不请求任何人帮忙了。"这次小鸟父母很担心地说:"这次真的是完了!"那些小鸟说:"奇怪!怎么会这样呢?前两次我们说他们会请亲戚朋友来、请他们的孩子来帮忙收割,你们都很开心,说不会有事;这一次我们说他们要靠自己,自己去收割,你们为什么那么震惊呢?"然后小鸟父母说:"你们有所不知,假如靠自己的话,他们真正会去做。靠别人当然不行,现在他们决定要靠自己,那么他们一定会做的,所以我们以后没东西吃了,我们最好搬走,搬到别的农场去。"

最
寓言
Zui Fable

---

[1] lark n. 云雀,百灵鸟

[2] fledgling n. 羽毛初长的雏鸟,刚会飞的幼鸟

[3] predict v. 预言,预报,预料

[4] definitely adv. 明确地,干脆地

The Boy and the Huge Rock

This story happened in a small mountain village about five hundred years ago. One day there was an earthquake. Nothing was destroyed and no one was hurt. But a huge rock fell from a nearby mountain and stopped in the middle of a road.

When the earthquake stopped, many people came to the road and saw the huge rock. Some of the strongest men tried to lift the rock out of the road. But they couldn't move it. They tried to push it but failed. They tried to pull it with ropes but nothing worked.

"Well," they all agreed, "There's nothing we can do about it. We'll have to change the road."

At this time a boy of 12 years old said, "I think I can help you to move the rock."

"You?" they shouted, "What are you talking about?" The men all laughed at the boy.

The next morning some people came into the road. One of them shouted, "The rock is gone!" More people ran out to see. It was true. The rock wasn't in the road any more. It wasn't even near the road.

"This is impossible," they said, "Where did it go?"

The boy stood on the road, smiling, said, "I told you I could move it last night."

The boy walked over to the place where the rock had been and uncovered some earth. "I buried it," he said. The people looked surprised.

"You see," he said, "I dug a deep hole next to the rock and I dug a small incline up to the rock, so the rock rolled down into the hole by itself. I covered it with earth."

The crowds shouted, "What a clever boy!" And some of them said, "Why haven't we thought of this good method?"

男孩和巨石

　　故事发生在约五百年前的一个小山村。有一天,那里发生了一次地震,当时没造成人员伤亡和财产损失,只是有一块巨石从附近的山上滚下,停落在一条大路的中央。

　　地震停止后,有许多人来到那条路上观看巨石。一些壮汉企图把巨石搬走,可是搬不动;想把它推开,却推不动;大伙用绳子拉它,也没有成功。

　　"唉,"他们齐声哀叹,"真是拿它没办法,那就只有改道了。"

　　这时有个12岁左右的孩子发言了:"我想我能帮助你们挪开这个大石头。"

　　"你?"大家不约而同地喊道,"你在说啥?"他们嘲笑起这个孩子来。

　　第二天一大早,人们来到街上,其中有个人高声喊道:"大石头不见了!"他立刻找来了众人观看。真的哟! 路上没有石头了,即使附近也没有。

　　"这不可能,"他们说,"它上哪儿去了?"

　　那个12岁左右的孩子也站在街上,微笑着说:"昨晚我告诉过你们我可以把它移走。"

　　于是他来到那巨石曾经停放之处,铲起一点松土,然后说:"我把它埋了。"人们都十分惊讶。

　　"你们看,"他说,"我先在石头旁边挖了一个深坑,然后又挖了一条通向石头的小小坡道,那石头就自己滚进了这个深坑,最后我用土把它埋实。"

　　众人不禁喊道:"好聪明的孩子!"还有些人说:"我们怎么没有想到这个好办法呀?"

The Crow and the Water Jug[1]

One day a crow was feeling very thirsty and looking for water. It had not rained for a long time. The sun had been shining hot and bright over the earth for many days. Everything was dry and hot. The rivers and ponds had all dried up too.

The thirsty crow flew all over the place looking for water. She felt so weak and tired from not having had any water to drink for many days. If she could not find water soon, she would die of thirst.

At last she flew down back to the ground, too tired to move her wings any more. While she was standing in the shade, waiting to die, she saw an old water jug nearby. The weak crow hopped over slowly to the water jug, hoping to find some water there. When she peeped over the mouth of the jug, she saw a little water at the bottom of the jug!

How happy the crow was when she saw this! She eagerly pushed her beak into the jug and tried to drink the water. However, the water level was too low in the jug. But the crow's beak was not long enough to reach it.

The crow thought of pushing the jug over on its side, but she knew that the water would only run out of the jug and seep[2] into the ground. Then she would have nothing to drink. The crow looked around very sadly. She had at last found water but she could not drink it.

She looked at the pebbles[3] lying beside the jug and suddenly she had an idea. With her beak, she began to pick up the pebbles one by one. She dropped each pebble into the water jug. As the pebbles piled up in the water jug, the level of water rose.

At last the water level was high enough for the crow to reach with her beak. The crow quenched her thirst, and flew away happily.

乌鸦喝水

久旱无雨的一天,一只乌鸦感到非常口渴,正在寻找水源。烈日正当空,炽热的阳光照射大地,到处显得干燥和酷热,河流和池塘也干涸了。

这只口渴的乌鸦飞了好多地方,仍然找不到水,觉得非常虚弱和疲劳。她已有几天没喝到水了,再找不到水的话,就要渴死了。

最后,乌鸦飞回地面,再也无力展翅飞翔了,只好站在一个荫凉处等死。就在这时,她发现附近有个陈旧的水瓶。虚弱的乌鸦慢慢地移向水瓶,希望瓶里有水。当她从瓶口往下看时,发现瓶底有水!

当乌鸦看到水时,她高兴极了,急忙把嘴伸入瓶内,希望能够喝到水。可惜,瓶里水位太低了,乌鸦根本碰不到水。

乌鸦想把水瓶推倒,但又怕水流了出来渗入泥土里,那样就无水可喝了。乌鸦觉得很颓丧,明明看到水了,却喝不到。

这时,她看到地面上的小石子,忽然心里有了主意。她开始用嘴一粒一粒地衔起小石子,丢入水瓶内。随着瓶中石子的堆砌,水位升高了。

等到水位升到她的嘴能够到,乌鸦喝到水了。乌鸦解了渴,高兴地飞走了。

---

[1] jug n. 壶,罐

[2] seep v. 渗透,渗漏

[3] pebble n. 卵石,砾石

Weakness or Strength?

Once upon a time, a 10-year-old boy decided to study judo[1] despite the fact that he had lost his left arm in a devastating car accident.

The boy began lessons with an old Japanese judo master. The boy was doing well, but he couldn't understand why, after three months of training, the master had taught him only one move.

"Master," the boy finally said, "shouldn't I be learning more moves?"

"This is the only move you know, but this is also the only move you'll ever need to know," the master replied.

Not quite understanding, but believing in his teacher, the boy kept training.

Several months later, the master took the boy to his first tournament[2].

To his surprise, the boy easily won his first two matches. The third match proved to be more difficult, but after some time, his opponent became impatient and charged; the boy deftly[3] used his one move to win the match. Still amazed by his success, the boy was now in the finals.

This time, his opponent was bigger, stronger, and more experienced. For a while, the boy appeared to be overmatched. Concerned that the boy might get hurt, the referee called a time-out. He was about to stop the match when the master intervened[4].

"No," his master insisted, "let him continue."

Soon after the match resumed, his opponent made a critical mistake: he dropped his guard. Instantly, the boy used his only move to pin him. The boy had won the match and the tournament. He was the champion.

On the way home, the boy and his master reviewed every move in each and every match. Then the boy summoned the courage to ask what was really in his master's mind.

"Master, how could I win the tournament with only one move?"

"You won for two reasons." the master answered, "First, you've almost mastered one of the most difficult moves of judo. Second, the only known defense for that move is for your opponent to grab your left arm."

The boy's biggest weakness had become his biggest strength.

弱还是强

从前,有一个10岁大的男孩子在一次惨烈的车祸中失去了左臂,但他仍然决定学习柔道。

男孩拜一位年长的日本柔道大师为师。孩子练得很好,但他不明白,训练3个月之后,师傅还是始终只让他重复同一个动作。

"师傅,"男孩终于忍不住问道,"我是不是可以学点儿别的动作了?"

师傅回答说:"这是你惟一知道的动作,但也是你惟一需要知道的动作。"

男孩虽然不理解,但他信任自己的师傅,于是继续练。

几个月后,师傅带这个男孩去参加他的第一次联赛。

令这个男孩不可思议的是,他很轻松地赢了头两场比赛。第三场比赛似乎更难,但过了一段时间他的对手开始失去耐心,向他冲过来,而这个男孩灵巧地用他学过的惟一一招击败了对手。尽管男孩对自己的成功感到惊讶,但是他还是进入了决赛。

这一次,他的对手更壮、更强,也更有经验。有那么一阵,男孩似乎抵挡不住了。考虑到男孩可能会受伤,裁判叫了暂停。他正准备停止比赛的时候,男孩的师傅阻止了他。

"不能停,"他说,"让他继续比。"

比赛继续进行之后不久,男孩的对手就犯了一个致命的错误:防漏(柔道术语)。男孩迅速用他那惟一的一招绊倒了对手,赢得了这场比赛和一个联赛,最终取得了冠军。

回家的路上,当男孩和他的师傅重温着每一场比赛里的每一个动作时,他终于鼓起勇气去问师傅是怎么想的。

"师傅,我怎么会用一个动作就赢了所有的比赛呢?"

"你获胜有两个原因。"师傅回答道,"第一,你已经基本掌握了柔道当中最难学的一个动作。 第二,要对付这个动作,你的对手惟一可以做的就是去抓住你的左臂。"

男孩最大的弱点变成了他最强的优势。

---

[1] judo n. 柔道

[2] tournament n. 锦标赛,联赛

[3] deftly adv 灵巧地,熟练地,敏捷地

[4] intervene v. 插入,干涉,调停

The Fox and the Sick Lion

The king of the beasts was ill. All day he lay curled up in his dark cave. He would be sighing and groaning, and giving faint tired-sounding roars whenever anyone came near him.

The other animals did not know what to do. Usually the Lion made all the decisions, so now they were afraid of doing the wrong thing. At last, however, they agreed that the best thing to do was to visit him in his cave. If they stayed away, he would certainly be angry; obviously, he was obviously too ill to harm them even if he wanted to.

One by one, sometimes in small, humble groups the animals made their way to the royal cave. Some took him presents—the best bit of meat they could find, or a bunch of fresh herbs[1]. Others just went to talk politely about the weather. Large and small, they all made their way to the cave.

Only one stayed away: the Fox.

After some time the Lion noticed that the Fox hadn't visited him. He sent a jackal[2] to look for him, to find out why he was being so rude.

"Fox," said the jackal, "His Majesty the Lion is not at all pleased with you. There he is lying dangerously ill in his cave and you have not even put your nose inside to ask how he is feeling. What excuse can you give for this disgraceful behavior?"

"Jackal," replied the Fox seriously, "It is not that I do not want to see the king. I respect him as much as anyone, and several times I came right to the cave mouth with my best piece of chicken, too."

"Well?" asked the jackal impatiently.

"Well, when I got there, I noticed something that made me much frightened to go any farther, though I want to see the king anxiously. I saw lots of footprints in the sand, footprints of many different kinds of animals. The strange thing was that they were all going one way into the cave. There was no sign of any footprints coming out. This made me think very carefully, I can tell you."

The Fox was right. The Lion was not ill at all, but thought of a way of saving himself a lot of troubles. Believing he was weak and harmless, the animals he usually had to hunt for food were all coming right into his cave and ended up as next meal.

"So you see why I shall not be calling on His Majesty." said the Fox.

狐狸和生病的狮子

百兽之王生病了,他整天蜷缩在黑暗的山洞里。只要有动物走近,他就唉声叹气、不断地呻吟,还发出疲倦而微弱的吼声。

动物们不知如何是好,平日都是由狮子发号施令,所以现在他们很怕自己会做错事。最后,大家商议决定,到山洞里去探望狮子是最明智之举。如果他们远远地躲着他,他一定会非常生气;显然,他病得不轻,就算想伤害他们,恐怕也没有力气了。

动物们轮流来探望狮王,有时也一小群一小群地来到他的山洞。有的还拿着礼物——能觅到的最好的肉或一把新鲜的药草;有的只是礼节性地谈一下天气。大大小小的动物都去过山洞了。

只有一个没来过,就是狐狸。

过了一段时间,狮子发现狐狸还没来探望过他。于是,就派豺去找狐狸,问他为什么如此不尊重他。

"狐狸,"豺说,"狮子陛下对你非常不满。他重病卧于洞中,但你却连句问候的话都没有,如此无礼之举你怎么解释呢?"

"豺,"狐狸一本正经地说,"并不是我不想去看大王。和其他动物一样,我也很敬重他,有好多次我都带着最好的鸡肉到了洞口。"

"是吗?"豺不耐烦地问道。

"唉,我告诉你,我是很想见大王,但在洞口发现的一些情况使我犹豫了,半步都不敢靠近。我在沙地上发现了各种动物的脚印。可这些脚印都只朝一个方向——山洞,却根本没有从山洞出来,这令我很诧异,我必须好好考虑一下了。"

狐狸的想法是对的。狮子其实没生病,他只是想找一个省事的办法。他平时捕食的那些动物都对他身体虚弱深信不疑,认为他无力伤害他们,就到山洞来探望他,结果都成了他的美餐。

"因此,你明白了我为什么不去探望大王。"狐狸说。

[1] herb n. 药草　　　　　　　　　　　[2] jackal n. 豺

A Magic Ring

Once upon a time there lived a young farmer. He worked very hard, but was very poor. One day, when he was far from home in the forest, an old woman looking like a farmer came up to him and said, "I know you work very hard, but all for nothing. I shall give you a magic ring. It will make you rich, and your work won't be in vain; when you wear the ring on your finger and say what you wish to have, you'll have it at once. But there is only one wish in the ring, so think carefully before you wish."

The astonished[1] farmer took the ring given by that woman and went home.

In the evening he came to a big city. There he went to a merchant and showed him the magic ring.

When the merchant heard the astonishing story, he thought of a plan. He invited the farmer to stay in his house for the night. At night he came up to the sleeping farmer, took the ring carefully off the man's finger, and put on another ring for him, which looked exactly like the one he had taken off.

In the morning, after the farmer had gone away, the merchant ran into his shop, shut the door, turning the ring on his finger, and said, "I wish to have a hundred thousand pieces of gold." And down they came, on his head, shoulders and arms, like a rain of gold. The frightened[2] merchant tried to get out of the shop, but in vain. In a few minutes, he was dead.

When the farmer returned home, he showed the ring to his wife. "Take a look at this ring." he said, "It's a magic ring. It will make us happy."

The astonished woman could hardly say a word. "Let's try. Maybe the ring will bring us more land." she said at last.

"We must be careful about our wish. Don't forget there's only one thing that we may ask for." he explained, "Let's better work hard for another year, and we'll have more land."

So they worked as hard as they could, and got enough money to buy the land they wished to have.

Then the farmer's wife thought of asking for a cow and a horse. They had discussed the matter more than once. "My good wife," said the farmer, "we shall get a horse and a cow without the ring." They went on working hard for a whole year, and again bought the things they wished to have.

"What happy people we are!" said the farmer.

"I don't understand you." answered his wife angrily. "There's nothing in the world that we can't have, and still we spend days and nights working as hard as before, because you don't want to use your magic ring."

"Stop talking about that ring." answered the farmer, "We are young and strong. Let's better wait till we are old. Then we may really need our magic ring."

Thirty, then forty years had gone by. The farmer and his wife had grown old. Their hair became as white as snow. They were happy and had everything they wanted. Their ring was still there. Although it was not a magic ring, it had made them happy.

魔戒

从前有一个年轻的农民。他干活很卖力气,却非常贫穷。有一天,当他远离家乡到森林去时,一个看上去像农民模样的老太太走到他身边说:"我知道你干活很卖力,却一无所获。我要送你一枚魔戒。它会使你富起来的,这样你的努力就不会白费了。你将这枚戒指戴到手指上并说出你想要什么,你马上就会有的。可是,这枚戒指只能实现一个愿望,所以在你许愿之前要仔细想好。"

这个农民吃惊地接过农妇送给他的戒指回了家。

晚上,他来到一座大城市。在那里,他去见了一位商人,给那人看了那枚魔戒。

当那个商人听说了这个令人吃惊的故事后,他就心生一计。他邀请那个农民到他的房子里过夜。夜里,他来到那个睡着的农民身边,小心翼翼地从那人的手指上取下戒指,然后将另一枚戒指戴了上去。这枚戒指看上去跟他取下来的那枚完全一样。

第二天早上,那个农民走后,那个商人就跑进店里,关上门,将那枚戒指戴在手指上说:"我希望我有10万块金子。"随后,金子就像金雨一样落在他的头上、肩上和臂上。那个吓坏了的商人竭力想从商店里跑出来,但无济于事。没几分钟,他就死了。

那个农民回到家里,把那枚戒指给妻子看。"看看这枚戒指,"他说,"这是一枚魔戒。它会使我们幸福的。"

那个吃惊的女人几乎说不出一句话来。"我们试试吧。也许这枚戒指能给我们带来更多的土地,"她最后说道。

"我们对我们许的愿一定要小心。别忘了我们能许的愿只有一个,"他解释说,"我们再好好苦干一年,就会有更多的土地。"

于是,他们尽其所能地努力干活,然后就得到足够的钱买了他们想拥有的土地。

随后,那个农民的妻子想要一头奶牛和一匹马。他们不止一次地讨论过这个问题。"我的好妻子,"那个农民说,"没有这枚戒指,我们也会拥有一匹马和一头奶牛的。"他们继续苦干了整整一年,然后又买了他们想要的东西。

"我们是多么幸福的人啊!"那个农民说。

"我不明白你的意思,"他的妻子生气地答道,"世界上我们想要什么就能有什么,可我们还是像以前那样没日没夜地苦干,因为你不想使用你的魔戒。"

"别提那枚戒指了,"那个农民回答说,"我们都年轻力壮。我们最好等到老了再说吧。到那时,我们也许真正需要那枚戒指。"

转眼三四十年过去了。那个农民和妻子已经老了。他们的头发变得像雪一样白。他们非常幸福,拥有了他们想要的一切。他们的那枚戒指还在那里。尽管那不是一枚魔戒,可是,它使他们过上了幸福的日子。

---

[1] astonished adj. 惊讶的　　　　　　　　[2] frightened adj. 受惊的,担惊受怕的

Stand in the Proper Position

Accidentally, a lily seed dropped in the wheat field. The seed budded[1], shot out the slender stems and leaves, grew the buds and bloomed the pure white flowers. Looking at the ordinary wheat around, the lily was proud: "Look, you're all ordinary wheat seedlings and your value is to yield several ears of wheat and become the food of mankind. As for me, I'm the noble lily, who is the symbol of purity, so you all can't compare with me ..."

The lily was so pleased with itself while the wheat seedlings remained silent. At this moment, a farmer went over. He took no interest in flowers. He only had the crops in his eyes, so the beautiful lily was only a weed to him. He pulled out the lily right away and threw it off on the ridge of the field.

The lily was insolated[2] by the scorching sun and gradually withered.

I believe you are excellent and the people around you are not so good as you. Perhaps you are a lily, but are you wrong to grow in the wheat field? The lily growing in the wheat field is a weed. You'd better consider in earnest where your proper position is.

最
寓言

Zui Fable

---

[1] bud vi. 发芽 n. 蓓蕾，叶芽   [2] insolate v. 暴晒

找到适合你的位置

　　一粒百合花籽,意外地落在麦田里。花籽发芽了,抽出了修长的茎和叶,又孕育出了花蕾,开出了洁白的花。看到周围都是普普通通的麦苗,百合十分骄傲:"看看你们,都是凡俗的麦苗,你们的价值也就是结出几穗麦子,成为人类的食物。而我呢,是高贵的百合,是纯洁的象征,你们谁都不能跟我相提并论……"

　　百合洋洋自得,麦苗们却一言不发。这时,一个农夫走了过来。他对花卉没有兴趣,眼里只有他的庄稼。美丽的百合对于他来说,不过就是杂草。他马上拔掉百合,扔在田埂上了。

　　百合被烈日暴晒着,渐渐枯萎。

　　我相信你很优秀,你周围的人都比不上你。也许你是一株百合,但你是不是错长在麦田里了? 长在麦田里的百合,就是杂草。还是认真想一下适合自己的位置在哪里吧。

The Donkey and the Salt

There was once a merchant who kept a donkey. They travelled all over the countryside, buying and selling different kinds of things. Sometimes the merchant would sell cloth and beads. At other times he would sell fruit and fresh vegetables. In fact, he would sell anything if he could make a bit of money out of it.

One day he heard that salt was sold cheaply at the seaside.

"I can get a fine price for that in the villages in the mountains." he thought and set off with his donkey to buy some.

The salt was certainly very cheap so that the merchant bought a good supply and loaded it on the donkey's back. All went well until they came to a narrow rocky bridge in the mountains with a deep stream flowing through it. The merchant was leading the donkey carefully along a slippery[1] ledge when suddenly the donkey lost his footing and slipped heavily into the stream.

As the donkey struggled to swim against the current, the water melted the salt he was carrying and washed it away, leaving only the empty bags fixed to the saddle. With no weight to pull him down, the donkey easily reached the bank and continued cheerfully on his way.

Soon afterwards the merchant decided to buy another load of salt. Once more he took his donkey to the seaside, loaded him up and set off for the mountains. As soon as they came to the narrow rocky bridge, the donkey remembered how easily he had lost his heavy load and how pleasant it had been travelling without it. This time he slipped into the stream on purpose and stayed struggling in the water until the salt had quite melted away.

The merchant was not at all pleased. He had lost two good loads of salt, and he suspected that the donkey had played a trick on him. He thought of a way to play a trick on the donkey in return.

The next time he went to the seaside, he bought a great load of sponges[2]. The donkey set off happily.

"These bags are light," he thought, "and by the time I pass the rocky bridge they will be lighter still."

Before long, they came to the rocky ledge. Once again the donkey rolled himself into the water and lay there struggling, waiting for the load to melt away as it had done twice before.

Instead of melting away, however, the sponges quickly soaked[3] up the water.

"What's this?" thought the donkey as he felt the bags getting heavier and heavier on his back. "Something is wrong here." Then as he felt himself sinking lower and lower in the stream, he yelled, "Help, master, help!"

The merchant bent over and pulled him gasping and spluttering out of the water.

"We'll go home now, shall we?" said the merchant. And he led the dripping donkey on up the mountainside.

"Now I have doubled the load I started with." thought the donkey sadly as he plodded[4] toward the village.

驴和盐

从前,有个商人养了一头驴。他走遍了所有的村镇,买卖各种东西。有时卖布匹和珠子,有时卖水果和新鲜蔬菜。事实上,只要能赚上点儿钱,他可以卖出任何东西。

有一天,他听说盐在海边卖得很便宜。

"我可以把盐贩到山村里卖个好价钱。"他想,便带上驴出发去买盐。

盐确实很便宜,商人买下了很多,安置在驴的背上。一切都进行得很顺利,直到他们来到山里一座狭窄的小石桥上，桥下有一条很深的小溪流过。商人牵着驴小心翼翼地走在光滑的石桥上，突然，驴一失足，重重地滑入小溪里。

当驴子挣扎着趟过溪流时，水溶化并冲走了他驮的盐，只留下空空的袋子系在鞍上。没有重物压着他，驴子轻松地到了岸边，愉快地接着赶路。

不久以后，商人又决定去买盐。他又一次带着驴到了海边，然后让驴子驮着盐向山里出发了。当他们再次经过那条狭窄的小石桥时，驴子很快就记起来上次如何轻松地卸掉了重负，并且想起没有压力赶路又是怎样地轻快。这次，他故意滑进了溪水中，在水中挣扎着，直到盐完全溶化掉。

商人很恼怒，他损失了两批盐，怀疑驴在跟他耍阴谋。于是，他想了一个办法也来戏弄驴。

再次去海边时，他买了一大袋海绵，驴子开心地出发了。

驴想，"这些口袋很轻，等过了那座石桥后就会更轻了。"

不久，他们来到了石桥。驴子又一次滚进了水里，并在那里挣扎着，等驮着的东西溶化掉，就像上两次那样。

然而，海绵非但没有溶化，反而很快吸满了水。

"为什么会这样？"驴子感到背上的口袋越来越沉，心想，"不对呀。"后来当他觉得自己在小溪里不住地往下沉时，便大声叫道："救命，主人，救命啊！"

商人弯下腰，喘着粗气，水花四溅地将驴拖了出来。

"现在，我们回家好吗？"商人说。全身湿透了的驴被牵着向山腰走去。

"现在驮的东西比刚驮时重了一倍。"驴子难过地想道，他拖着沉重的步子缓慢地朝村子走去。

---

[1] slippery adj. 滑的，光滑的

[2] sponge n. 海绵，海绵体

[3] soak v. 浸，泡

[4] plod v. 沉重缓慢地走；辛勤工作

The Swallow and the Other Birds
燕子和其他的鸟

It happened that a countryman was sowing some hemp[1] seeds in the field where a swallow and some other birds were hopping about picking up their food.

"Beware of that man." said the swallow.

"Why, what is he doing?" asked the others.

"Those are hemp seeds he is sowing; be careful to pick up every one of the seeds, or else you will repent it."

The birds paid no heed to the swallow's words.

By and by the hemp grew up and was made into cord[2]. Of the cords nets were made, and many a bird that had despised the swallow's advice were caught in nets made out of that very hemp.

一个庄稼人正在地里播种大麻种子。一只燕子和一些其他的鸟正在那里寻找食物。

"小心那个男人。"燕子说。

"为什么？他在干什么？"其他鸟问。

"他正在播种大麻的种子，一定要仔细地把每一粒都拣出来，否则你们会后悔的。"

鸟儿们都没在意燕子的话。

大麻渐渐长大了，后来被搓成了绳子，绳子又被结成了网。许多对燕子的劝告满不在乎的鸟儿正是被这张用大麻编成的网捉住的。

---

[1] hemp n. 大麻；纤维　　　　　[2] cord n. 绳索；束缚

Precious Hands

There was once a shepherd who had a daughter whose great beauty attracted a lot of young men from all over the country to propose to her.

One day, the shepherd asked his daughter, "My dear daughter, tell me, what kind of man do you want to be your husband?"

His daughter said, "My dear father, my future husband can be poor but also a wealthy man."

"How could that be, poor and rich are two opposite things!" said her father curiously.

"Dear father, a poor person also has his wealth." said his daughter.

The shepherd then announced that his daughter was ready for marriage.

One day, there were many eligible[1] men gathering outside the shepherd's home. He came out and said, "All right, gentlemen, those who think they are eligible, please come forward and tell me your qualifications[2]!"

A few well-dressed gentlemen came forward followed by their servants and loads of gifts carried by camels. "We are rich men; we have gold and silver mines, silk, fur and red carpets. Please choose one of us to be your husband."

The shepherd's daughter just smiled.

Then came five young men holding some jewelry boxes. "These golden boxes contain rare jewelry. You will be the most wealthy person if you choose one of us to be your husband."

"None of you is my idea of an ideal husband." said the disappointed lady.

One by one, the young men came forward, but they were all rejected by her. The shepherd began to worry. Suddenly, a plainly dressed young man appeared.

The shepherd asked, "Young man, you look so poor. What treasure can you offer my daughter?"

"My wealth is always with me, and it is my hands." the young man said, "I am a good tailor. I am also a good carpenter. I can make tables and chairs within an hour. Moreover, I can also put up a tent for you all!"

The lady smiled. The young man continued, "I can cook, too. I can cook delicious meals. However, I do not have any property, servants or jewelry. But, with my pair of hands, I do have a whole life of wealth!"

"That's great!" shouted the shepherd's daughter excitedly. "You are more wealthy than any of them because you have a pair of precious hands. You are my idea of an ideal husband!"

A pair of hardworking hands can create infinite wealth.

宝贵的双手

从前,有个牧羊人,他有一个非常美丽的女儿,她的美吸引了方圆几百里的年轻小伙子,他们慕名前来求婚。

一天,牧羊人问女儿:"孩子,告诉父亲,你想要什么样的人做你的丈夫呢?"

女儿回答说:"亲爱的父亲,我将来的丈夫是个既贫穷又富有的人。"

"这怎么可能呢?"牧马人好奇地说,"贫穷和富有是相对的啊!"

"亲爱的父亲,"女儿说,"贫穷的人也有他自己的财富。"

然后,牧羊人就发出了招婿的通告。

一天,许多有心的求婚男子云集在牧马人居住的帐篷外面。牧羊人走出帐篷,对大家说:"好,有心来求婚的人士,请上前来说说自己的条件吧!"

几个衣着华丽的小伙子首先走上前来,他们的仆人牵着满载礼品的骆驼跟在后面。"我们都是有钱人。我们拥有金山银山、丝绸、羊毛和红毡。请从我们当中选一个做你的丈夫吧。"

牧羊人的女儿只是报以微笑。

接着,五位手捧珠宝盒子的小伙子走上前来。"这些金盒子里装满了稀世珍品。如果你选择我们其中之一作为你的丈夫,你将成为最富有的人。"

"你们都不是我心目中的理想丈夫。"牧羊人的女儿失望地说。

小伙子们一个个走上前来求婚,但都被她拒绝了。牧羊人开始着急起来。突然,有个衣着朴素的青年走了过来。

牧羊人问:"年轻人,你看上去很穷啊。那么,你有什么宝物要献给我女儿吗?"

"我的财富一向随身携带,它就是我的双手,"青年说,"我是一个技艺精湛的裁缝师;我还是一个熟练的木匠,我能在一个小时内,给你们制造一套桌椅;而且,我还能给你们搭一个帐篷。"

牧羊人的女儿笑了。"我还会烹饪,"青年继续说,"我能煮出最美味的饭菜。然而,我既没有什么财产,也没有仆人,更没有什么金银珠宝。但我有一双手,有了这双手,我就拥有了一生用之不尽的财富!"

"太好了!"牧羊人的女儿激动地高声喊道,"你比他们中的任何人都富有!因为你有一双宝贵的手,你正是我心目中的理想丈夫。"

一双勤劳的手,可以创造无限的财富。

[1] eligible adj. 有……资格的　　　[2] qualification n. 资格,资历

第三章

智慧箴言
Words of Wisdom

Sand and Stone

The story goes that two friends were walking through a desert. During some point of the journey they had an argument, and one friend slapped the other one in the face. The one who got slapped was hurt, but without saying anything, he wrote in the sand: "Today my best friend slapped me in the face."

They kept on walking until they found an oasis[1], where they decided to take a bath. The one who had been slapped got stuck in the mire[2] and started drowning, fortunately, his friend saved him. After he recovered from the near drowning, he immediately wrote on a stone: "Today my best friend saved my life." The friend who had slapped and saved him asked, "After I hurt you, you wrote in the sand but now you write on a stone. Why?" The one who wrote replied: "When someone hurts us, we should write it down in the sand where winds of forgiveness can erase it away. But when someone does something good for us, we must engrave[3] it on a stone where no wind can ever erase it."

Learn to write your hurts in the sand and to carve your benefits in the stone.

---

[1] oasis n. （沙漠中的）绿洲

[2] mire n. 泥沼，困境

[3] engrave v. 雕刻

沙子和石头

故事说的是两个好朋友一起穿越一个沙漠。途中他们为某事起了争执,其中一个人一巴掌扇在另外一个人的脸上。被扇的那个人感到受到了伤害,但他什么也没有说,只是在沙子上写道,"今天我最要好的朋友打了我一个耳光。"

他们继续走下去,发现了一片绿洲,于是他们决定洗个澡。先前被打的那个人这时不小心陷入泥沼,已经开始下沉,幸运的是他的朋友把他给救了出来。他苏醒过来后,立刻在一块石头上写道,"今天我最要好的朋友救了我一命。"于是,扇过他耳光又救过他性命的朋友问他"在我打了你之后,你把它记在了沙子上,而现在你却记在石头上,为什么呢?"写字的那个人回答说:"当我们被别人伤害了之后,我们应该把它写在沙子上,这样,宽容的风很快就会将其抹去,但当我们受到别人的帮助之后,我们必须将它刻在石头上,这样,风就不会轻易把它磨灭。"

学会将你所受到的伤害写在沙子上,把别人给予你的帮助记在石头上。

The Shipwreck of Simonides

A learned man has always a fund of riches in himself.

Simonides, who wrote such excellent lyric[1] poems, the more easily to support his poverty, began to make a tour of the celebrated cities of Asia, singing the praises of victors for such reward as he might receive. After he had become enriched by this kind of gain, he resolved to return to his native[2] land by sea; for he was born, it is said, in the island of Ceos.

Accordingly he embarked on a ship, which a dreadful tempest, together with its own rottenness, caused to wreck at sea. Some gathered together their girdles, others their precious effects, which formed the support of their existence. One who was over-inquisitive, remarked, "Are you going to save none of your property, Simonides?" He made reply, "All my possessions are about me."

A few only made their escape by swimming, for the majority[3], being weighed down by their burdens, perished. Some thieves too made their appearance, and seized what each person had saved, leaving him naked. Clazomenae, an ancient city, chanced to be near; to which the shipwrecked persons repaired. Here a person devoted to the pursuits of literature, who had often read the lines of Simonides, and was a very great admirer of him though he had never seen him, knowing from his very language who he was, received him with the greatest pleasure into his house, and furnished him with clothes, money, and attendants. The others meanwhile were carrying about their pictures, begging for victuals. Simonides chanced to meet them; and, as soon as he saw them, remarked, "I told you that all my property was about me, what you have endeavoured[4] to save is lost."

---

[1] lyric adj. 抒情的

[2] native adj. 出生地的

[3] majority n. 大半，大多数

[4] endeavour v. 努力做某事

西莫尼狄斯遇难记

一个有学问的人往往身怀无穷的财富。

西莫尼狄斯所写的抒情诗美誉天下，因此他轻而易举就摆脱了贫困之苦。他开始游历亚洲各地名城，一路走来以歌颂胜利者的丰功伟绩来获取报酬。通过这种途径发家后，他决定乘船返回家乡，据说他出生在西奥斯岛。

于是他便乘船出发了。可怕的是途中遭遇了暴风雨，而船本身又很破旧，所以他们的船被狂风巨浪打翻了。同船的行人中有的收拾着细软什物，有的则收拾着仅供赖以生存的值钱财物。有一个非常好奇的人问道："西莫尼狄斯，难道你不打算保住自己的财产吗？"西莫尼狄斯答道："我就是自己的全部财产。"

只有少数人游泳逃生，而大多数人由于负担过重而被淹死。一些强盗也趁火打劫，抢走了逃生人的所有东西，连衣服也抢了个精光。附近有一座名叫克赛佐门纳的古城，所有的逃生者都逃到了那里。那儿有一个热爱文学的人，经常研读西莫尼狄斯的诗歌。虽然他与西莫尼狄斯未曾谋面，却狂热地崇拜着他。他从西莫尼狄斯的言谈举止中得知他的身份，于是备感荣幸地请他到自己家里，给他衣服、金钱和随从。而此时，其他的遇难者只能背井离乡，沿街乞讨。西莫尼狄斯偶然遇到他们时，说："我告诉过你们，我所有的财富就是我自己，而你们竭尽全力去保护的东西却丢光了。"

最 寓言
Zui Fable

The Old Woman and the Doctor

An old woman having lost the use of her eyes, called in a doctor to heal[1] them, and made the bargain with him in the presence of witness that if he should cure her blindness, he should receive from her a sum of money; but if her infirmity[2] remained, she should give him nothing. This agreement being made, the doctor, time after time, applied his salve[3] to her eyes, and every visit took something away, stealing all her property little by little. And when he had got all she had, he healed her and demanded the promised payment. The old woman, when she recovered her sight and saw none of her goods in her house, would give him nothing. The doctor insisted on his claim, and as she still refused, summoned[4] her before the Judge.

The old woman, standing up in the Court, argued: "This man here says the truth in what he says, for I did promise to give him a sum of money if I should recover my sight; but if I continued blind, I was to give him nothing. Now he declares that I am healed. I, on the contrary, affirm[5] that I am still blind; for when I lost the use of my eyes, I saw in my house various chattels and valuable goods; but now, though he swears I am cured of my blindness, I am not able to see a single thing in it."

---

[1] heal v. 治愈，病愈

[2] infirmity n. 疾病，病症

[3] salve n. 药膏，软膏

[4] summon v. 召唤，传唤

[5] affirm v. 断言，重申

老太婆与医生

有位患了眼病的老太婆，请来一位医生给她治病，并在证人面前谈定：如果医生能把老太婆的瞎眼治好，那么他将从她那里得到一笔钱；如果老太婆的病毫无起色，那么他将得不到任何报酬。达成协议之后，那位医生每次来给她敷药治疗时，总是趁她看不见，顺手牵羊地偷走一些东西。渐渐地，他偷光了老太婆的所有财产。当他把老太婆所有的东西都拿走时他将她治好了，他向老太婆要他们约好的报酬。而老太婆呢，当她的视力恢复后，发现她屋子里什么都没有了，便准备什么都不给他。医生坚持索要，而她依旧拒绝。于是医生将她叫到了法官面前。

老太婆站在法庭上，说道："这位男士说的是实话，因为我曾经许诺，如果他把我的眼睛治好，我会给他一笔钱；如果治不好，他将不会得到任何的报酬。现在他声称治好了我的眼睛，相反，我肯定我还是瞎的。因为在我眼睛没瞎的时候，我看到我房子里有各种财物和值钱的家业，但是现在，虽然他发誓治好了我的眼睛，我还是看不到房子里的任何东西。"

Flower in the Desert

This story happened many, many summers ago.

There was a young flower in the desert where all was dry and sad-looking... she was growing by herself ... enjoying everyday... she said to the sun: "When shall I be grown up?" And the sun would say: "Be patient[1]—Each time I touch you, you grow a little..." And she was so pleased. Because she would have a chance to bring beauty to this corner of sand... And this is all she wanted to do—bring a little bit of beauty to this world.

One day, a hunter[2] came by—and stepped[3] on her. She was going to die—and she felt so sad. Not because she was dying—but because she would not have a chance to bring a little bit of beauty to this corner of desert.

The great spirit saw her, and heard her. Indeed, he said... she should be living...He reached down and touched her, and gave her life.

And she grew up to be a beautiful flower... And this corner of the desert became more beautiful because of her.

---

[1] patient adj. 忍耐的, 耐心的　　　　[3] step v. 践踏

[2] hunter n. 猎人

沙漠之花

这个故事发生在很久很久以前的一个夏天。

在一个到处都充满着干燥与衰败景象的沙漠中，盛开着一朵小花……她孤零零地生长着……享受着每一天……她对太阳说："我何时才能长大呢?"太阳回答说："不要着急——我的光芒每触碰你一次，你就会长大一点儿……"小花听了非常高兴。因为她可以有机会为这片沙漠增添一处美丽的风景了……这就是她想要做的一切——为这个世界带来一点儿美丽。

一天，一个猎人路过这里——从她身上踏了过去。她就要死了——她感觉到如此悲伤。她之所以悲伤，并不是因为她将要死去，而是因为她再也没有机会为这片沙漠增添一处美景了。

一个伟大的精灵看到了她，并听到了她的诉说。事实上，他说……她应该活下去……于是，他来到沙漠上抚摸着她，并赐予了她生命。

后来，她终于长成了一朵美丽的花儿……这片沙漠的角落也因她的存在而变得更加美丽。

The Crow that Wanted to Be Swan

Once upon a time, there was a crow. He hated his black feathers. He thought that people disliked him because of his black feathers.

One day the crow saw a swan flying in the air. He was fascinated[1] by the swan's white feathers. He thought that he could also become white if he lived like the swan.

The crow said to himself, "The swan is white because he always swims and dives in the pond."

From that day onwards, the crow began to swim and dive in the pond. Sometimes, he felt it wasn't enough, so he also washed his feathers thoroughly[2] with water, hoping that his blackness could disappear.

The swan was surprised to see this. He said to the crow, "Hey, Crow! You are not used to the water. You will get sick if you swim and dive in the water too long."

"I will get used to the water soon." answered the crow. "Then my feathers will be as white as yours."

The crow soaked[3] himself everyday for a long time, but his feathers did not turn white; he only became weaker and weaker. Finally, he fell sick and died.

---

[1] fascinate v. 强烈地吸引，迷住   [3] soak v. 浸，泡
[2] thoroughly adj. 十分地，彻底地

想变成天鹅的乌鸦

从前,有一只乌鸦,他讨厌自己黑色的羽毛,他觉得人们之所以不喜欢他,都是因为他黑色的羽毛。

有一天,乌鸦看见一只天鹅从天空中飞过,对天鹅白色的羽毛羡慕不已。他想,要是能像天鹅那样生活,他的羽毛也可以变成白色。

乌鸦对自己说:"天鹅之所以是白色的,就是因为他每天都把自己浸泡在湖水里。"

从那天开始,乌鸦就浸在湖里,有时觉得还不够,拼命地泼水、洗涮,希望能将黑色褪去。

天鹅看见了,觉得很奇怪,就对乌鸦说:"乌鸦,你不谙水性,如果你长时间待在湖水里会生病的。"

"不久我就会习惯了,"乌鸦说,"到那时,我的羽毛就能跟你一样白了。"

乌鸦每天都把自己浸泡在湖水里很长时间,但是他的羽毛依然没有变成白色。他自己却一天天地愈发虚弱,终于重病而亡。

The Donkey and Its Shadow

A traveler wanted to hire a donkey to go to town which was quite a distance away. It so happened that someone was willing to hire out a donkey, and the traveler agreed to the offer.

The owner of the donkey said to the traveler, "This animal is very lazy. I have to rush it with a stick all the time to make sure it moves. Otherwise, it will waste you a lot of time. I suggest that we go together. You can ride on the donkey's back while I follow behind to rush it. When we arrive at the town, I can ride it home."

Both parties agreed to the arrangement[1] and they started off on the journey. The sun was scorching heat but the plan went well with the traveler riding the donkey and the owner himself following behind.

At noon, they couldn't stand the heat anymore, so they decided to stop and have a rest. The traveler alighted[2] from the donkey and sat in its shadow to stay away from the sunlight.

"Oh, no," said the owner, "this is my donkey. You are not allowed to sit in its shadow."

"But I hired it from you," argued the traveler, "so I deserve[3] the right to sit in its shadow."

The owner said, "You hired the donkey all right, but you did not hire its shadow! The shadow belongs to me!"

They two ended up quarrelling[4] and fighting at the dusty road under the scorching heat of high noon. Bored by their long-time fight, the donkey ate some grass and then ran off, leaving the two quarrelling men behind. It ran farther and farther, at last out of the version of the traveler and its owner. Now its shadow doesn't belong to anyone. The donkey is running with its shadow.

驴和他的影子

有个旅客想到城里去,可是路途太遥远了,他想租一头驴来代步。刚好,有个人愿意将驴出租给他。旅客也同意了他提出的报酬。

驴的主人对旅客说:"这头驴很懒,我必须时时刻刻拿着棍子在它身旁赶着,它才肯走。否则,耽误了你的时间就不好了。所以我建议跟你一起走,你骑在驴背上,我在后面赶着它。到了城里,我还可以把它骑回来。"

双方都同意了,然后他们就上路了。太阳高挂,旅客骑驴,驴的主人赶驴,一路相安无事。

到了中午,由于太热了,他们决定停下来休息一会儿。旅客下了驴,坐在驴子的影子里,躲避阳光。

"噢,这样不行,"驴的主人说道,"这是我的驴,所以你不可以坐在它的影子里。"

"可是这驴是我租下的啊!"旅客争论道,"所以我才有权利坐在它的影子里。"

驴的主人说道:"你是租了我的驴没错,可是你并没有租下它的影子,所以它的影子还是属于我的!"

他们争论不休,甚至大打出手。完全不理会身在尘土飞扬的路上、烈日当头的正午时分。他们争了好久,驴吃了一会儿草,丢下两个争吵的人,自己跑掉了。驴越跑越远,终于离开了旅客和主人的视线,现在它的影子不属于任何人,只有它和它的影子一同上路。

---

[1] arrangement n. 安排,筹备

[2] alight v. 下车

[3] deserve v. 应受,应得,值得

[4] quarrel n. 争吵,吵架

The Travelers and the Wallet

One day two travelers were passing a place. Suddenly, one of them saw a wallet on the ground. He picked up the wallet and said, "Oh, what a lot of money! I am very lucky today!"

"Don't say 'I', but say 'we'. We should share whatever we find in the journey." said his friend.

The one who picked up the wallet didn't agree with his friend's opinion. He said, "I am the one who found the wallet, so I should keep it. It is 'mine', not 'ours'."

"But 'we' found the wallet together while we were traveling," argued[1] the other traveler.

"'I' found the wallet and picked it up. Isn't that right?" the first traveler insisted[2] that he should keep the wallet.

Suddenly, when they were arguing, a group of people ran towards them and shouted, "Thieves! Thieves!"

When the traveler who had found the wallet heard the shout, he cried, "We are in danger!"

"No, no. Don't say 'we are', say "I am" in danger!" said the other traveler, and he ran away.

In the end, the traveler who had found the wallet was caught by the people.

---

[1] argue v. 争辩,争论　　　　　　　　　[2] insist v. 坚持,坚决认为

旅客和钱包

有一天，两个旅客经过一个地方。忽然，其中一个人发现地上有个钱包，连忙捡了起来。他打开一看，说："哇！里面有这么多钱！今天我真幸运！"

他的朋友说："不要说'我'，要说'我们'。我们应该分享我们旅途中发现的所有东西。"

捡到钱包的这个人不同意他的朋友的说法。他说，"钱包明明是'我'捡到的，所以应该我保管它，它是'我的'，而不是'我们的'。"

"但这是'我们'两个人旅行时一起发现的啊！"另一个人争论道。

"是'我'发现并捡起了钱包。难道不是吗？"第一个旅客坚持认为钱包应该归他所有。

正在他们争论的时候，忽然远处涌出一群人，正朝着两个人冲来，喊道："捉贼啊！捉贼啊！"

捡到钱包的人说："不好了，我们遇到麻烦了！"

"不,不,别说'我们'，说'我'遇到麻烦了！"另一个旅客说，之后就跑开了。

最后那个捡到钱包的人被那群人抓住了。

The Three Ants

As a man lay sleeping in the shade of a tree, three ants climbed onto his nose.

After greeting each other, one of them said, "these are the most infertile hills and plains I have ever seen in my whole life. I have searched for the whole day, but cannot find even a grain of cereal[1]."

The second ant said, "I haven't discovered anything either, though I have looked in every corner. I dare say this is the so-called 'drift sand' known by our clan[2]."

The third ant held up his head and said, "My friends, we are standing on a super giant[3] ant's nose. This ant has extraordinary power. He is too large for us to see his whole body. His body stretches so far that we cannot finish traveling on it. His voice is so loud that we listen but hear nothing. He is boundless!"

When the third ant was speaking, the other two ants looked at each other and burst out laughing. At that moment, the man changed a posture, raised his hand and wiped his nose. The three ants were crushed to death in one minute.

---

[1] cereal n. 谷类
[2] clan n. 宗族

[3] giant n. 大力士, 巨人

三只蚂蚁

树阴下有个男子在躺着睡觉,他的鼻梁上爬着三只蚂蚁。

这三只蚂蚁碰在一起后,蚂蚁甲说:"这些山丘和平原是我平生所见过的土地中最贫瘠的。我找了一整天,却连一粒谷子也没有看见。"

蚂蚁乙说:"我也是什么都没有发现,我已找遍了每一寸土地的每一个角落。我敢说,这就是我们族群称为'流沙'的那种荒地。"

蚂蚁丙昂起头来说:"朋友们,我们现在是站在一只超级大蚂蚁的鼻子上。这是只神力无穷的大蚂蚁,他的身躯庞大到我们极目而不见其全貌;他的身影辽阔到我们遍游而不逾其边际;他的声音洪亮到我们闻所未闻。他是杳无边际的啊!"

当蚂蚁丙在大发高论的时候,蚂蚁甲、蚂蚁乙相视一下,然后大笑起来。这时候,那个男子换了个睡姿,抬起手在鼻子上抹了一把,三只蚂蚁转瞬间被碾得粉碎。

The Golden Chain

Once upon a time, there was a poor fisherman who always dreamed of becoming rich. He wished to become a millionaire, and so did his wife.

He had heard from some old men before, that several ships loaded with diamonds and gold had once sunk in the nearby sea water. Because of this, for a long time he kept searching that whole area for this treasure.

One day, he went fishing. While he was sitting in the boat daydreaming, he suddenly felt that the fishing rod was being weighed down by a heavy object. He excitedly pulled hard at it, and what he saw made him exclaim, "Wow! A big, shiny golden chain!"

He excitedly pulled hard at the golden chain to get it into the boat, but there seemed to be no end of it. His boat started to get over-loaded because of the weight of the golden chain, and the sea water filled his boat. However, he had begun dreaming of a big house, a big piece of land, and buying horses and cows...

He kept pulling in the chain though the boat kept sinking[1]. The boat was finally submerged[2], and he struggled to stay afloat. Unfortunately his feet were entangled[3] in the golden chain and he drowned.

---

[1] sink v. 下沉，沉没

[2] submerge v. （使）没入水中

[3] entangle v. 使纠缠，使混乱，卷入

金链

很久以前,有个贫穷的渔夫,总是梦想发财,他希望自己成为百万富翁,他妻子更是如此。

他曾听一些老人讲过,过去有几艘载满金银珠宝的船只沉没在这附近的海域里。因此,长期以来,他一直在这一带的海域里搜寻着,希望能打捞到一些金银珠宝。

有一天,他出海捕鱼,当他坐在船上想入非非时,忽然感到钓线被非常沉重的东西拖住了。他一下兴奋起来,使劲地往上拉鱼线,当鱼线拖出水面时,他不禁大声尖叫起来:"哗!金光闪闪的长金链!"

他喜出望外,拼命地把金链往船上拖,可是金链很长,似乎没有尽头。由于金链很重,小船严重超载,海水灌进了船内。然而,他却依旧做着没完没了的黄粱美梦:我可以买一幢大房子,置一大片稻田,再买下几头牛、几匹马……

尽管小船一直往下沉,他却依然贪心地拖着金链。最后,小船终于沉下去了。他在水中拼命挣扎想游出水面,然而不幸的是,他的双脚被金链缠住了,结果他被淹死了。

The Camel[1] and the Wild Boar's Debate

There was once a camel who quarreled endlessly with a wild boar.

The camel said, "Being tall is the best. It makes me high above the rest."

The wild boar replied, "A short body is the best. I can easily escape from any enemy."

"Why don't we get someone to judge that?" said the camel. "Whether being tall or being short is better." The wild boar agreed.

They passed a botanic[2] garden surrounded by low hedges[3]. The camel stood by the side of the hedge and started eating the plants there as his lunch.

He laughed at the wild boar, saying, "See, being tall is good!"

The wild boar, standing outside the wall, could not even see the beautiful scenery[4] in the garden.

Soon they came to another botanic garden. It had high walls but there was a small door for entrance. The wild boar entered through the small door while the camel was left behind as it was too low for him to go through.

The wild boar enjoyed himself, eating the plants in the garden. When he came out of the garden, he laughed at the camel, "Now, what do you think about that? Is being tall better or being short better?"

Both of them then looked at each other and said, "Whether being tall or short, each has its own advantages." They no longer needed anyone to be a judge of that.

[1] camel n. 骆驼

[2] botanic adj. 植物的，植物学的

[3] hedge n. 树篱

[4] scenery n. 景色，风景

骆驼与野猪的辩论

一只骆驼和一只野猪正在争论不休。

骆驼说："身材高是最好不过的了，可以感觉自己高高在上。"

野猪说："身材矮才是最好的，容易躲开敌人的视线。"

"不如我们去找别人评评理？"骆驼说。"看看是高的好，还是矮的好，如何？"野猪答应了。

他们走近一个植物园，这里的四周围着矮墙。骆驼站在墙边，将长颈伸入墙内，吃了不少植物，把他的午餐解决了。

然后骆驼嘲笑野猪说："没错吧？长得高好！"

野猪正站在墙角下，连园子里的美景都错过了。

不久，他们又经过另一个植物园，这里的四周围着高墙，但却有一个供出入的小矮门。野猪从小门钻进去了。骆驼因个子过高无法进去，只好站在园外。

野猪在园里吃着植物，吃得非常痛快。当走出园子时，他嘲笑骆驼说："现在你认为高的好，还是矮的好？"

两只动物互相望了一眼，同时说道："高有高的好处，矮有矮的好处。"所以，他们不用去找别人评理啦！

A Circle Missed a Wedge
缺了楔子的圆圈

Once a circle missed a wedge. The circle wanted to be whole, so it went around looking for its missing piece. But because it was incomplete, it could roll only very slowly. It admired the flowers along the way. It chatted with worms. It enjoyed the sunshine. It found lots of different pieces, but none of them fit. So it left them all by the side of the road and kept on searching. Then one day the circle found a piece that fit perfectly. It was so happy. Now it could be whole, with nothing missing. It incorporated[1] the missing piece into itself and began to roll. Now that it was a perfect circle, it could roll very fast, too fast to notice the flowers or talk to the worms. When it realized how different the world seemed when it rolled so quickly, it stopped, left its found piece by the side of the road and rolled slowly away.

从前有一只圆圈缺了一块楔子。圆圈想保持完整，便四处寻找失去的那块楔子。由于它不完整，所以只能很慢地滚动。一路上，它对花儿露出羡慕之色。它与蠕虫谈天说地。它还欣赏到了阳光之美。圆圈找到了许许多多不同的配件，但是没有一件能完美地与它相配。所以，它将它们统统弃置路旁，继续寻觅。终于有一天，它找到了一个完美的配件。圆圈是那样地高兴，现在它可以说是完美无缺了。它装好配件，然后滚动起来。既然它已成了一个完整的圆圈，所以滚动得非常快，快得以至于无暇观赏花儿，也无暇与蠕虫倾诉心声。圆圈快奔急骋，发现眼中的世界变得如此不同，于是，它不禁停了下来，将找到的那个配件留在路旁，又开始了慢慢地滚动。

---

[1] incorporate v. 把(某事物)并入，包含

The Marble[1] Tile and the Marble Statue
地砖与雕像

One night, a marble tile in a museum talked with a marble statue.

"Marble statue, it's just not fair! Why does everybody from all over the world come all the way here just to admire you while stepping on me? We are from the same cave. Not fair!"

"My dear friend, do you remember the day when the designer[2] tried to work on you? You resisted the tools because you were afraid of the pain. He couldn't work on you, so he worked on me instead. I knew that I would be something different after his efforts, so I bore all the painful tools he used on me ... My friend, there is a price for everything in life. Since you decided to give up halfway, you can't blame anybody who steps on you now."

一晚，博物馆里的大理石地砖与大理石雕塑像攀谈起来。

"大理石雕塑，真不公平！为什么这全世界的人千里迢迢跑到这里来瞻仰你，我却被踩在脚下？我们可是来自同一个洞穴呢。真不公平！"

"我的朋友，你还记得设计师想对你进行加工的那天吗？因为你害怕工具给你带来的痛苦，设计师无法对你进行加工，所以只好由我来代替你。我知道经过他的改造之后，我就会不同以往，所以我忍受着他用在我身上的所有工具给我带来的痛苦……朋友，生命中的任何事情都是要付出代价的。既然你在途中选择了放弃，那么，你也就别再责怪他人把你踩在脚下了。"

---

[1] marble n. 大理石   [2] designer n. 设计者, 构思者

The Cat that Reformed

A cat wore a priest frock to show that she wanted to become a nun[1]. She wrote a letter to the mice which read: "Killing is cruel. From today onwards, I am not willing to do anything that will hurt others, because I am a nun now."

The mice replied: "Although you now pose as a person of high morals[2], we still don't believe you. Our lessons in history are clear in our minds."

The cat wore a ragged cloth and applied flour all over her body. The mice saw her and said, "You damned, no matter how humble[3] you pretend to be, we can see your fierce nature through it."

The cat then adopted another strategy. She jumped up to a wooden nail on the wall. She hung herself at the bottom of the wooden nail and pretended to be dead.

One of the mice, secretly coming out from the hole, saw her and said, "What a pity you are dead. But even that cannot change your reputation[4] for having a sinister and cunning nature."

The mice were not fooled by the cat from the beginning to the end, because they know the "nature" of the cat.

[1] nun n. 修女, 尼姑

[2] moral n. 道德, 品行

[3] humble adj. 谦虚的, 谦恭的

[4] reputation n. 名誉, 声誉

洗心革面的猫

一只猫,穿上了道袍,以表示她要出家做尼姑了。她写信给老鼠说:"残杀是一件残忍的事,我呢,从今以后,不再干流血的事件了,因为我已经出家为尼了。"

老鼠回信道:"虽然如今你道貌岸然,我们却依然不会相信你的,因为历史的教训在我们的脑海里根深蒂固。"

猫穿上一件破衣服,用面粉涂满全身。老鼠们见了,说:"可恶的猫,你伪装得再好,我们也能透过你肮脏的破衣服,看到你凶恶的天性。"

于是,猫又想出另一个计谋,她跳上一枚钉在墙上的木钉,用双脚把自己倒挂在木钉上,假装死了。

有一只老鼠偷偷地钻出洞口看见了她,说:"可怜的死猫,但即使那样,我们却还是不能相信你已经改掉了阴险狡诈的本性。"

老鼠们始终没有上猫的当,因为他们深知猫的本性。

The Two Donkeys

A wild donkey once met a tame[1] donkey feeding on a hillside. The wild donkey was thin and small. He spent his life out of doors, sheltering as best he could in the cold weather and eating the sparse[2] hill grass all the year around. He sometimes had to walk miles to find fresh water and at night there was always danger from prowling wolves. They threatened his life while hunting for food.

The tame donkey was sleek[3] and fat. During the summer he fed on the rich meadow grass while in winter he was given corn and hay to eat. There was always a pail of fresh water for him to drink and at night he was shut safely in a stable.

"How lucky you are," said the wild donkey , "I wish I could live like you."

A few days later the wild donkey was once more foraging on the hillside. Looking down he saw the tame donkey walking slowly along the road, carrying a heavy load of wood. As he watched, the tame donkey paused to snatch at a thistle[4] growing by the roadside. Immediately his driver began to shout at and beat him with a stick.

"I've changed my mind about your way of life," thought the wild donkey, "I see that you have to pay heavily for the corn and hay they give you."

---

[1] tame adj. 顺服的, 柔顺的

[2] sparse adj. 稀少的, 稀疏的

[3] sleek adj. 圆滑的

[4] thistle n. [植]蓟

两头驴

一次，一头野驴看到一头家驴在山坡上吃草。生活在野外的野驴又瘦又小，天气寒冷时，他还得努力找个较好的藏身之处，山上零星的小草就是他整年的食物。有时，为了找到干净的水源解渴，他不得不跑到几英里远的地方。晚上还要警惕狼群，他们到处觅食会威胁到自己的生命。

可那头家驴却肥肥壮壮的。夏天，牧场里丰美的鲜草可以任他享用；冬天，他可以吃到谷物和干草；他总可以喝到新鲜的水，晚上他可以在牲口棚里安心地过夜。

"你太幸运了，"野驴说，"我真想过你的那种生活。"

数天后，野驴又来山坡吃草。他俯身向下望去，正看到家驴驮着沉重的木头，缓慢地沿着路边走着。家驴想停下来吃路边的蓟草，赶驴人马上对他大吼，并用棍子抽打他。

"我不要过你那样的生活了，"野驴心想，"我终于知道了，你必须要付出沉重的代价才能得到他们的谷物和干草。"

A Round Plate in the Sky

The cock and the owl started an argument[1] just after the sun had set.

The cock said, "There is a shining round plate in the sky, releasing its hot energy to the world. Once it rises up in the sky, the weather becomes warmer."

The owl refuted the cock's statement and said, "You are wrong. The shining round plate never releases[2] hot energy. It becomes cooler after it comes out."

The cock said, "Nonsense, I am quite sure it is the source of hot energy. I have already experienced it personally so far these days."

The owl said, "You are the one who talks rubbish[3]! When it comes out, I never feel hot at all. I feel cold instead."

In fact, their argument about this subject is irrelevant[4]. Most of the cock's activities are carried out during the daytime, and the round shining plate he sees is the sun. The owl, however, only comes out at night, so to him the round plate is the moon.

---

[1] argument n. 争论, 争吵
[2] release v. 释放
[3] rubbish n. 胡说八道, 废话
[4] irrelevant adj. 不相干的, 不重要的

挂在空中的圆盘

太阳下山后,公鸡与猫头鹰之间的舌战开始了。

公鸡说:"空中亮闪闪的圆盘,给大地送来了热量。只要它一升上天空,天气就变得暖和起来。"

猫头鹰反驳说:"你错了,天上那亮亮的圆盘根本不放热,而且往往它出来以后,天气就更冷了!"

公鸡说:"胡说!我坚信它是热源!这是几天来我所亲身体验到的。"

猫头鹰说:"你才是瞎说呢!它出现的时候,我一点儿也没觉得热,反而觉得凉快得很。"

其实,他们的争论根本就是牛头不对马嘴。公鸡大部分的活动时间在白天,他见到的亮闪闪的圆盘是太阳;猫头鹰却只在夜里出门,他见到的圆盘是月亮。

The Naughty Kangaroo[1]

There was a small Kangaroo who behaved badly in school. He put thumbtacks on the teacher's chair. He threw spitballs[2] across the classroom. He set off firecrackers[3] in the lavatory and spread glue[4] on the doorknobs[5].

"Your behavior is unbearable!" said the school principal, "I am going to see your parents. I will tell them what a problem you are!"

The principal went to visit Mr. and Mrs. Kangaroo. He sat down in a living-room chair.

"Ouch!" cried the principal, "There is a thumbtack on this chair!"

"Yes, I know." said Mr. Kangaroo, "I enjoy putting thumbtacks on chairs."

A spitball suddenly hit the principal on the nose.

"Forgive me." said Mrs. Kangaroo, "But I can never resist throwing those things."

There was a loud booming sound from the bathroom.

"Keep calm." said Mr. Kangaroo to the principal, "The firecrackers that we keep in the medicine chest have just exploded. We love the noise."

The principal rushed to the front door. In an instant he was stuck to the doorknob.

"Pull hard." said Mrs. Kangaroo, "There are little globs of glue on all of our doorknobs."

The principal pulled himself free. He dashed out of the house and ran off down the street.

"Such a nice person." said Mr. Kangaroo, "I wonder why he left so quickly."

"No doubt he had another appointment." said Mrs. Kangaroo, "Never mind, supper is ready."

Mr. and Mrs. Kangaroo and their son enjoyed their rich evening meal. After the dessert, they all threw spitballs at each other across the dining-room table.

淘气的袋鼠

有一只小袋鼠总在学校里惹是生非。他把图钉放到老师的椅子上,把纸团扔得满教室都是,在卫生间放鞭炮,还把胶水涂在门把手上。

"你的行为简直让人难以忍受!"校长说:"我要去见你的父母,把你的表现和他们说说!"

校长去拜访了袋鼠夫妇。他在客厅的椅子上坐下。

"哎哟!"校长叫了起来,"椅子上有图钉!"

"对,我知道,"袋鼠先生说:"我喜欢在椅子上放图钉。"

突然,一个纸团飞来正中校长的鼻子。

"抱歉,"袋鼠夫人说:"我总是不由自主地乱扔东西。"

一声轰响从盥洗室传来。

"不必紧张,"袋鼠先生对校长说:"放在药箱的鞭炮爆炸了,这种声音我们都很喜欢。"

校长匆忙地走向前门,手马上被门把手给粘住了。

"用力拉,"袋鼠夫人说:"我们家所有门的把手上都涂有胶水。"

校长终于挣脱了,他从房子里冲了出去,沿路跑了。

"挺好的一个人,"袋鼠先生说,"不知他为什么坐这么一会儿就走了。"

"一定是有别的约会,"袋鼠夫人说,"没关系,我们准备吃晚饭吧。"

袋鼠夫妇和儿子一起享受起了丰盛的晚餐。吃完甜点后,他们在饭桌旁互相扔起纸团来。

---

[1] kangaroo n. 袋鼠

[2] spitball n. 纸团

[3] firecracker n. 鞭炮,爆竹

[4] glue n. 胶水

[5] doorknob n. 门把手

Lion and Gnat[1]

The lion with the gnat puts on a cold contempt[2]. The gnat is filled with rage[3]; he can not stand the slight. The gnat then rises in arms and sallies forth to fight. He's a knight and bugler, too; he trumps with all his breath, and challenges his foe to fight him to the death.

The lion laughs; but gnat's not jesting. On the back, or eyes, or ears, our trumpeter[4] comes fast, picks out his spot, and waits for his chance; with eagle's swoop[5] he lunges, and in the back his sting he plunges.

The lion quivers: at the foe his tail he flaunts. But nimble is our gnat. Besides he knows no fear. Full on the forehead perched, he is sucking near the brain. The lion twists his head; the lion shakes his mane; our hero strikes and strikes again. Gets home upon the nose, or pricks behind the ear. How lion swore! How terrible his roar!

He grinds his teeth with foaming jaws; He tears the earth up with his claws. The forest shakes all around, with those awful tones to hear; The beasts are terror-struck; they hide and fly in fear, as if the flood had come, or some great conflagration. And who makes all this? A gnat has thrown them in this consternation.

The lion's rage is spent, his frantic efforts cease; he falls upon the ground and sues the gnat for peace. The gnat has slaked his ire[6]; his ardor he restrains. Achilles part is played: its Homer's now remains; his own, the trump that to the woods shall make his triumph known.

---

[1] gnat n. 蚊子

[2] contempt n. 轻视,蔑视

[3] rage n. 狂怒,盛怒

[4] trumpeter n. 号兵,喇叭手

[5] swoop n. 飞扑,突然袭击

[6] ire n. 发怒,怒火

狮子和蚊子

一只狮子对蚊子摆出一副冷冰冰的轻蔑态度。蚊子十分恼火,他忍无可忍,于是就武装起来,冲出去要与狮子决一死战。蚊子既是武士又是号手,于是就憋足气吹起号角,向他的敌人宣战,一决高低。

狮子狂笑起来,然而蚊子可没开玩笑。我们的号手在狮子的后背、眼睛和耳朵上发动攻击。他瞄准地方,抓住机会,像雄鹰似地猛扑下来。对准狮子的后背狠狠地刺进去。

狮子扭动着身体,甩着尾巴抽打他的敌人。但蚊子十分敏捷,而且浑身是胆,毫不畏惧。他在狮子的前额上疯狂地吸吮,马上就要吸到脑子里了。狮子摇头晃脑,甩动着鬃毛。我们的英雄发动一次又一次的猛烈进攻,一会儿钻进他的鼻孔,一会儿叮咬他的耳朵。狮子开始咒骂吼叫!吼叫声十分恐怖!

他口吐泡沫咬紧牙关,用爪子在地上乱抓乱刨。这种可怕的吼声震颤着整个森林,野兽们惊慌失措——有的藏起来,有的害怕得飞走了,纷纷逃离了森林,像是遭遇水火的侵袭。那么,究竟是谁搞得大家如此惶恐不安呢?原来只是一只小小的蚊子!

狮子被蚊子折磨得筋疲力尽,他停止了挣扎,瘫倒在地上向蚊子求和。蚊子报了仇,平了心头之气后也就息怒了。蚊子的阿喀琉斯英雄角色上演完毕。他正以大诗人荷马的姿态,飞回森林宣扬自己的胜利去了。

The City Mouse and the Country Mouse

最
寓言
Zui Fable

Once there were two mice. They were good friends. One mouse lived in the country; the other mouse lived in the city. After many years, the country mouse saw the city mouse; he said, "Do come and see me at my house in the country." So the city mouse went. The country mouse took him to his home in a field[1], and took out all the best food to the city mouse. The city mouse said, "This food is not good, and your house is not good. Why do you live in a hole in the field? You should come and live in the city. You would live in a nice house made of stone. You would have nice food to eat. You should come and see me at my house in the city."

The country mouse went to the house of the city mouse. It was a very good house. Nice food was set ready for them to eat. But just as they began to eat they heard a great noise. The city mouse cried, "Run! Run! The cat is coming!" They ran away quickly and hid.

After some time they came out. When they came out, the country mouse said, "I do not like living in the city. I like living in my hole in the field, for it is nicer to be poor and happy than to be rich and afraid."

---

[1] field n. 田地，牧场

城里老鼠和乡下老鼠

从前,有两只老鼠,他们是好朋友。一只老鼠居住在乡村,另一只住在城里。很多年以后,乡下老鼠碰到了城里老鼠,他说:"你一定要来我乡下的家看看。"于是,城里老鼠就去了。乡下老鼠领着他到了自己那个在田地上的家里。他把所有最精美食物都找出来给城里老鼠。城里老鼠说:"这东西不好吃,你的家也不好,你为什么住在田野的地洞里呢? 你应该搬到城里去住,你能住上用石头造的漂亮房子,还会吃上美味佳肴,你应该到我城里的家看看。"

乡下老鼠就到城里老鼠的家去。房子十分漂亮,好吃的东西也为他们摆好了。可是正当他们要开始吃的时候,听见很大的一阵响声,城里的老鼠叫喊起来:"快跑! 快跑! 猫来了!"他们飞快地跑开躲藏起来。

过了一会儿,他们出来了。当他们出来时,乡下老鼠说:"我不喜欢住在城里,我喜欢住在田野我的洞里。因为这样虽然贫穷但是快乐自在,比起虽然富有却要过着提心吊胆的生活来说,要好些。"

The Swan, the Barracuda[1] and the Prawn[2]
天鹅、梭鱼和大虾

One day, a swan, a barracuda and a prawn were trying to drag[3] a small cart together. They pulled and pushed with all their might, but no matter how hard they tried, the small cart remained immovable. Why was that? They could not understand what was wrong.

Actually, the cart was not too big or heavy. The reason was that while the swan was pulling the cart upwards to the sky, the prawn was stepping backwards and the barracuda was pushing it forwards. The three of them were moving in different directions, so the cart stayed still!

有一天,天鹅、梭鱼和大虾集合在一起,一块儿拉着一辆小车。他们卯足了劲儿,可是无论怎样拖啊,拉啊,推啊,小车还是停在原地,没有挪动半步。为什么会这样呢? 他们怎么想也想不通。

其实,并非小车太大太重,而是另有原因:天鹅使劲往上,向天空的方向直提;大虾则一步步向后倒拖;梭鱼却向前推。他们的方向不一致,小车当然还是停在原地了。

---

[1] barracuda n. 梭鱼

[2] prawn n. 大虾,对虾

[3] drag v. 拖,拉

The Carter[1] and Hercules
车夫和大力神

One day, a carter was driving his cart along a country road. The cart got stuck in the deep mud, but the foolish farmer made no effort to get it out. Instead he began to pray to the gods for help. The god Hercules finally appeared and told the man to get busy and push it. "Put your shoulder to the wheel, my man." Hercules advised, "Goad on your horses, and never pray to me for help any more, until you have done your best to help yourself, or depend upon it, you will henceforth[2] pray in vain[3]."

一名车夫赶着货车沿着乡间小路行进。途中车轮陷入了很深的泥中。这个笨车夫没有自己尝试把车拉出来，而是开始祈祷神灵帮助他。大力神终于来了，让他行动起来推车，并对他说："朋友，用你的肩膀扛起车轮，"大力神建议，"再抽打拉车的马，不要再光向我祈求了。如果你没有尽全力帮自己、自力更生，你以后再祈求也没有用。"

---

[1] carter n. 车夫

[2] henceforth adv. 从今以后

[3] in vain 徒劳的

Wait a Little Longer in Despair

An old woman grew a large patch[1] of corn behind her house.

A full corn said, "On the day of harvest, the old lady will certainly pick me first because I'm the best corn of this year!" But on the harvest day, the old woman didn't pick it.

"Tomorrow, tomorrow she will definitely pick me!" the best corn comforted itself. The next day the old woman got in some other corn but not the best one.

"Tomorrow, the old lady will surely pick me!" the best corn still comforted itself . But since then, the old woman never came until one day the best corn became disappointed. The original full grain became dried and hard, its whole body seemed to be cracking[2], so it prepared to rot with the corn stalk.

Just at this moment the old woman came. She said as she was picking it, "This is the best corn this year. As seeds, they will certainly grow better corns next year!"

Perhaps you're always very confident, but do you have the patience to wait a little longer when you're in despair?

[1] patch n. 一小块土地   [2] crack v. （使）某物裂开

绝望时再等一下

一个老婆婆在屋子后面种了一大片玉米。

一个颗粒饱满的玉米说道："收获那天,老婆婆肯定先摘我,因为我是今年长得最好的玉米!"可是收获那天,老婆婆并没有把它摘走。

"明天,明天她一定会把我摘走!"最棒的玉米自我安慰着。第二天,老婆婆又摘走了其他一些玉米,可惟独没有摘这个玉米。

"明天,老婆婆一定会把我摘走!"最棒的玉米仍然自我安慰着。可是,从此以后,老婆婆再也没有来过。直到有一天,玉米绝望了,原来饱满的颗粒变得干瘪坚硬。它看起来快要干裂了,于是它准备好与玉米杆一起腐烂了。

可是就在这时,老婆婆来了,一边摘下它,一边说:"这可是今年最好的玉米,用它作种子,明年肯定能种出更棒的玉米。"

也许你一直都很相信自己,但你是否有耐心在绝望的时候再等一下呢?

The Stork[1], the Lobster[2] and the Whale[3]

There was once an extraordinarily large stork. The stork himself thought there could be no other animal in the world that was bigger than him.

One day, the stork was flying leisurely above the sea. After some time, he felt quite tired and started to look for a place to rest. Unfortunately, there was nothing other than the water in the sea.

He suddenly noticed a big stick floating in the sea. He thought, "This stick is big enough for me to rest on." So he landed on the stick.

While resting there, the stork started to flick his feathers. Then he heard a voice, "Who are you? Why do you land here, on me?"

The stork replied, "I am the stork, the biggest animal in the world."

"Ha, ha! I am the lobster. Don't you know that you are resting on my antenna now? How can you say that you are the biggest in this world! This is really funny! Ha, ha, ha!"

The stork was speechless and he quickly flew away. The lobster looked at the stork in the sky, feeling very proud that he was truly the largest animal in this world.

While the lobster was swimming in the sea, he felt tired and wished to look for a place to rest. He saw a hole in front of him. "This is not bad, I'll take a rest here!" He stuck his body inside, leaving his head on the outside.

A voice suddenly boomed: "Hey, who is this? Why are you here?"

The lobster replied, "I'm the lobster, the world's largest animal. That's who I am!"

There was a loud laugh. "What! You are the largest? Let me tell you, I am the whale. You are now in my nostril[4]!" The whale suddenly sneezed[5] and sent the lobster up into the sky.

最
寓言
Zui Fable

鹳鸟、龙虾和鲸鱼

古时候，有一只长得特别大的鹳鸟。当时，他以为世界上没有比自己更大的动物了。

一天，鹳鸟在海上展翅飞翔，飞着飞着，不觉有点儿累了，想找一个地方休息，可是不幸的是在这片汪洋大海上，除了海水之外，似乎别无他物。

忽然，鹳鸟发现海面上有一根挺大的木棍，心想："嘿，这木棍不小，正好歇脚。"于是鹳鸟就飞落在那根木棍上面。

鹳鸟一边剔着羽毛，一边休息。这时，有个声音问："你是谁啊？怎么落到我这儿来啦？"

鹳鸟回答说："我是鹳鸟，是世界上最大的动物。"

"哈哈！我是龙虾，你现在不是在我的须子上休息吗？还说什么你是世界上最大的！真可笑，哈哈……"

鹳鸟说不出话，拍打着翅膀，飞走了。龙虾望着天空的鹳鸟，得意洋洋，他觉得自己才是世界上最大的动物。

龙虾在海上游逛着，后来游累了想找个地方歇息。他看见前边有个洞，心想到："这儿不错，就在这儿待会儿吧！"说着，就钻入洞里了，还把脑袋露在外边。

这时有个瓮声瓮气的声音问："喂，是谁啊？怎么在这儿待着？"

龙虾应着："是我呀，世界上最大的动物龙虾在此！"

于是响起一阵大笑，"什么，你最大？告诉你吧，我是鲸鱼。你现在是在我的鼻孔里！"说着，鲸鱼打了个喷嚏，一下把龙虾喷射到半空了。

---

[1] stork n. 鹳鸟

[2] lobster n. 龙虾

[3] whale n. 鲸鱼

[4] nostril n. 鼻孔

[5] sneeze v. 打喷嚏

The Eagle and the Crow

Deep in the jungle, a crow saw a little eagle practicing how to fly. The crow had never seen an eagle before.

He flew to the eagle and asked, "What kind of bird are you?"

"I am an eagle." said the little eagle.

"Oh, the humans always say that the eagle is the bravest among all birds. But why are you not better than me when you are flying?" The crow teased the eagle.

"I am a young eagle; my feathers are not fully formed and my wings are still weak."

"Even when you have grown-up feathers and a pair of strong wings, you will not be better than I." said the crow arrogantly before flying away.

One day, when the crow was flying low in the sky, a big bird suddenly flew down towards him and caught him. The crow cried while resisting, "Help! Help! What kind of bird are you? You are so big and strong!"

"Don't you remember? I am the little eagle that you once insulted[1]. Now I have grown up." While talking, the eagle seized the crow and took him away for a meal.

---

[1] insult v. 侮辱，辱骂

雄鹰和乌鸦

乌鸦飞到一座深山里，看见一只雏鹰正在练习飞翔。他从来没见过老鹰。

乌鸦飞到雏鹰跟前问道："你是什么鸟？"

"我是一只鹰。"小雏鹰说道。

"哎呀！人们常说雄鹰在飞禽中是最猛的一种鸟类，可是你飞起来却还不如我呀！"乌鸦揶揄道。

"我是雏鹰，羽毛还没有丰满，翅膀还不硬。"

"像你这个样子，就是羽毛丰满了，翅膀硬了，飞翔的本领也不会比我强到哪里去。"乌鸦傲慢地说道，然后飞走了。

有一天，乌鸦在空中飞得很低，突然，有一只大鸟向他猛扑过来，然后把他抓住了，乌鸦惊慌失措地一边挣扎，一边喊道："救命，救命！你是什么鸟，你怎么又大又强壮？"

"你忘啦？我就是上次被你嘲笑过的那只雏鹰，现在长大了！"说着，雄鹰把乌鸦带到山顶上饱餐一顿。

The Conceited Rabbit

Once a number of rabbits lived happily together in a jungle. Among them was a wise old rabbit who used to protect everyone, so the rabbits seldom face dangers.

One day the wise old rabbit called all the rabbits together to tell them something. He said, "There is a fierce[1] tiger in our area, roaming about looking for food. You should not leave your homes while the tiger is around."

The rabbits followed his advice. They never play on the grassland or eat in the area where the tiger appears. The tiger has been here for several days, but he doesn't find any animal. Feeling hungry, the tiger walks tiredly.

However, one day, a mischievous[2] young rabbit caught sight of the tiger. "The tiger looks thin and weak," thought the young rabbit. "I'm going to disturb him a bit to see whether he is really fierce."

The next morning, the rabbit came to the same place, crouching in the stones, waiting for the tiger. The tiger had actually noticed the young rabbit who was too far away to be caught. The tiger therefore pretended to ignore[3] him, and moved away.

Nothing happend. The third day, the young rabbit became braver. He tried to get closer to the tiger. The tiger still ignored him as he was not feeling hungry because of the long distance.

"The tiger is not really as fierce as the chief said," thought the young rabbit. "I'm sure I can safely approach him."

On the fourth day, the rabbit ate on the grassland. Fortunately, the tiger was full that day, so he didn't hurt the rabbit. The rabbit became more conceited, he said to himself, "The tiger doesn't hurt rabbits at all."

On the fifth day, as the tiger was resting quietly, the young rabbit confidently[4] approached him in a friendly manner. When the foolish young rabbit was close enough, the tiger caught hold of him and made a meal out of him.

When other rabbits heard about this, they are all frightened. The old rabbit sighed, "If the young rabbit had listened to me and didn't appear in the area where the tiger hunted, he wouldn't have died."

自以为是的兔子

从前,有一群野兔幸福地生活在大森林里,因为有一只聪明谨慎的首领老兔保护着他们,所以兔群中很少发生危险。

有一天,老兔召集所有的兔子来开会,告诫道:"我们这里出现一只凶猛的老虎,一直在附近出没寻找食物,当老虎在附近时,你们一定不要离开家。"

野兔们都很信服老兔。他们不再到草地上玩耍,也不到老虎出没的地方去吃草。老虎来到这个地方,好几天都没发现动物的踪影。他觉得肚子饿了,疲乏地走着。

有一只爱恶作剧的小兔在洞口看见了这只老虎,心想:"这老虎看上去又瘦又虚弱,我倒想试一试看他有多么凶猛。"

173

第二天一早,小兔又来到同样地方,他蹲在山石间等候老虎。出来觅食的老虎远远地就瞥见了他,由于距离太远,抓不到他,就装作漫不经心的样子走过去。

什么也没发生。第三天小兔就更大胆了。他试着离老虎更近一些。老虎远远地就看见了他,由于距离还是太远,所以依然不动声色地走过去。

小兔心想:"看来老虎不像首领说得那么可怕和凶猛。我肯定接近他没什么危险。"

第四天,他索性跑到草地上去吃草。幸运的是,老虎一早已吃饱了,也没伤害他。小兔更加得意了,对自己说:"老虎根本就不伤害兔子。"

于是,第五天,当老虎在静静地休息时,小兔便大摇大摆地走近老虎。当小傻兔离得足够近时,老虎扑上去就把他吃了。

野兔们知道后全吓坏了。老兔叹息说:"如果小兔乖乖听话,不在老虎守猎的地方出现,他是不会出事的。"

---

[1] fierce adj. 凶猛的,好斗的

[2] mischievous adj. 恶作剧的,爱搞蛋的

[3] ignore v. 忽视,不理

[4] confidently adv. 信赖地,安心地

The Shepherd Boy and the Wolf

There was once a shepherd boy in a village. Every day he took the sheep to the foot of a hill to graze[1]. The life was easy, but he was soon bored with his work.

One day when watching the sheep, the naughty shepherd boy decided to play a trick on the villagers. So he stood up and shouted, "Help! Wolf! Wolf!"

The villagers heard the shepherd boy's shouts. They ran to the foot of the hill carrying sticks and farm tools. To their surprise, they did not see any wolf. They could only see the shepherd boy who laughed at them. They asked, "Where is the wolf?" The shepherd boy replied, "There is no wolf. The grass blowed by the wind made me think the sound is a wolf."

The villagers were very angry. They went back to their fields.

The next day, the shepherd boy played the same trick on the villagers. The villagers heard him shouting. They ran to the foot of the hill to help.

The shepherd boy laughed again when he saw the villagers. "Just now one of my sheep jumped over the hay, so I thought it was a wolf. I made a mistake. Sorry!" The villagers were very angry but they could not do anything.

On the third day, the villagers heard the shepherd boy calling for help again. This time they thought the boy was joking again, so they did not bother to respond. They continued working in their fields.

However, this time a wolf had really come to attack the sheep. It caught and killed many sheep. The shepherd boy hid behind the tree and cried because he was very frightened. After the wolf had left, the shepherd boy told the villagers what had happend in tears.

At first, they didn't believe him.

The shepherd boy said, "I did joke on you before, but it's real this time!"

The villagers trusted him when they saw the dead sheep.

"You can't blame us, but blame yourself for lying and joking on others. No one believes you even when you tell the truth." said the villagers.

牧童和狼

从前村子里有个牧童,每天他把羊群赶到山脚下吃草,日子过得很轻松,但他很快觉得自己的工作无聊。

一天,当牧童在看守羊群时,调皮的他决定跟村民开个玩笑。他起身喊道:"救命呀!狼来了!狼来了!"

村民听到牧童的叫喊声,纷纷拿了锄头和棍子冲上来。奇怪的是,他们没有看见狼,只见牧童哈哈大笑。村民问:"狼呢?""没有狼,风吹茅草的声音让我以为是狼来了!"牧童答道。

村民很生气,他们回到地里。

第二天,牧童又开着同样的玩笑捉弄村民。村民又闻声赶来救命。

当看到村民时,牧童却大笑说:"刚才我的一只羊跳过茅草,所以我以为是狼。搞错了!对不起!"村民们很生气但他们却什么也做不了。

第三天,村民再次听到牧童的求救声。这次村民以为他又在开玩笑,于是对牧童的叫喊声置之不理,埋头工作。

然而,这一次狼真的来攻击羊了。它追赶着羊群,咬死了好多只羊。牧童非常害怕躲在树后吓得哭了起来。等到狼走后,牧童哭着把事情告诉村民。

起初,村民不相信他的话。

牧童说:"以前我的确开你们的玩笑,但这次是千真万确啊!"

村民看见遍地横死的羊才相信了他的话。

"你不能怪我们,要怪就怪你说谎和捉弄人,等你说真话时已经没人肯相信你了。"村民说道。

---

[1] graze v.（动物）吃草

The Two Gardeners

Two brothers who were both gardeners, had a piece of land for their inheritance[1], of which each cultivated a half; united by a strict kinship they had everything in common.

One of them, named John, of an inquisitive[2] mind and some oratorical[3] powers, thought himself a great philosopher; therefore John passed his time in reading the almanac[4], in observing the weather, the weathercock, and the wind. Presently, giving the rein to his sublime genius, he wished to discover how such millions of peas could be so quickly produced from a single one; and wherefore the seed of the linden, which produced a large tree, should be much smaller than the bean, which attained but two feet in height; and again, by what mysterious secret this bean, which was heedlessly sown in the earth, contrived to attain a proper position in its bosom, so as to shoot out a root below, while it elevated its stem above the surface.

While he was thus meditating and afflicting himself at not being able to penetrate these important secrets, he forgot to water his garden; his spinach[5] and lettuces died for want of moisture; the north-wind killed his fig-trees, which he neglected to cover up. No fruit was sent to the market, no money came to his purse, and the poor "philosopher", with his almanacs, had no resources but his brother.

The latter was at work from the first dawn of day, singing at the top of his lungs; he grafted, and watered everything, from the peach-tree to the currant bush, without caring to discover that those he could not comprehend. He continued to sow, in order that he might reap. Consequently his garden thrived to a miracle; he had money and fruit. When John, in astonishment came to ask him how he was so successful. "Brother," said he, "here is the whole secret: I work, and you reflect, which is more profitable? You are racking your mind, while I am enjoying myself; which of us is wiser?"

两位园丁

有两兄弟都是园丁，共同继承了一块土地，平分耕种。兄弟俩感情很好，一起分享所有的东西。

其中一个叫约翰，他对什么都好奇，且具有演讲才能，自诩为伟大的哲学家。所以，他终日研读历书，观测天象。不久前，他的旷世才情促使他异想天开，想探究一粒豌豆在一块地上如何能很快产出几百万颗豆子来；为什么可以长成参天大树的菩提树的种子竟然比只能长两英尺高的蚕豆的种子要小得多；又是哪股神秘的力量使得偶然撒播在土里的蚕豆，能找到合适的位置，生根发芽呢？

他就这么冥思苦想着，为这些疑惑不能解开而苦恼。他忘了给园子浇水，菠菜和莴苣都枯死了；没有被他"武装"起来的无花果树也经不起寒风的侵袭被冻死了。没有水果拿到市场上去卖，也就没有钱流进他的钱包里。这位潜心钻研的穷困"哲学家"不得不向兄弟求助。

而后者（他的兄弟），每天天刚破晓，就下地劳动，还时常引吭高歌。他给果树嫁接，为园子里的每株植物浇水，从桃树到小葡萄丛。对那些自己不理解的奥秘向来不屑一顾。为了有个好收成，他不停地耕种。结果，他的园子繁茂似锦，水果和钞票都有了。当约翰诧异地前来询问他如何获得成功时，他的兄弟却对他说："兄弟，我注重劳动，而你注重思考，你说谁收获更多呢？你在冥思苦想时，我却在享受生活，你说我们哪一个更聪明呢？这就是奥秘所在。"

---

[1] inheritance n. 继承，遗产

[2] inquisitive adj. 好追根究底的，过分好奇的

[3] oratorical adj. 演说的，雄辩的

[4] almanac n. 年历

[5] spinach n. 菠菜

Purgatory[1] May Be Paradise

A king was embarked[2] on board a ship, which also carded a slave. The boy had never been at sea, nor experienced the inconvenience of a ship. He set up weeping and wailing, and all his limbs were in a state of trepidation[3], however much they soothed him, he was not to be pacified. The king's pleasure was disconcerted by him, but they offered no help. On board that ship there was a physician. He said to the king, "If you will order it, I can manage to silence him." The king replied, "It will be an act of great favor."

The physician directed that they throw the boy into the sea, and after he had plunged repeatedly, they seized him by the hair of the head and drew him close to the ship, where he grabbed the rudder with both hands, scrambled up on to the deck, slunk into a corner and sat down quietly.

The king, pleased with what he saw, said, "What art is there in this?" The physician replied, "Originally he had not experienced the danger of being drowned, and undervalued the safety of being in a ship; just as a person is aware of the preciousness of health only when he is overtaken with the calamity[4] of sickness."

---

[1] purgatory n. 暂时的苦难

[2] embark v. 上船

[3] trepidation n. 颤抖

[4] calamity n. 灾难

苦痛与幸福

国王带着一个奴隶乘坐在一条船上。奴隶从未出过海,也从未经历过坐船之苦。他开始哭泣、悲嚎,四肢不停地颤抖。人们想尽办法安抚他,但他仍无法平静。国王原本愉快的心情被他搅得不安起来,但人们却束手无策。在船上有个医生,他对国王说:"如果您吩咐让我一试的话,我有办法让他平静。"国王说道:"那就太好了。"

医生吩咐他们把奴隶扔到海里,让他反复沉浮几次后,才抓住他的头发把他拖到船边。他双手紧紧抓住船舷,爬上甲板,缩到一个角落里坐下来,不再吭声了。

国王看到很满意,问道:"这是什么道理?"医生回答说:"先前他没有经历溺水的危险,所以不珍惜在船上的安全,就像一个人只有感受到病痛的折磨时,方知健康的可贵一样。"

Why Moths[1] Are Grey?

Moths were once the most beautiful in the animal kingdom. At one time they were more colorful than the butterflies. They had always been helpful, kind, and generous[2] creatures. One day the angels up in heaven were crying. They were sad because it was cloudy and they couldn't see the people on the earth. Their tears fell down to the earth as heavy rain. The sweet little moths hated to see everyone so sad. They decided to make a rainbow. The moths figured that if they asked their cousins, the butterflies, to help, they could all give up just a little bit of their colors and they could make a beautiful rainbow.

One of the little moths then flew to ask the queen of the butterflies for help. The butterflies were too vain and selfish to give up any of their colors for neither the people nor the angels. So the moths decided to try to make the rainbow by themselves. They beat their wings very hard and the powder on them formed little clouds that the winds smoothed over like glass. Unfortunately, the rainbow wasn't big enough so the moths kept giving a little more and a little more until the rainbow stretched all the way across the sky. They had given away all their color except grey, which didn't fit into their beautiful rainbow.

Now the once colorful moths were plain and grey; but the angels up in heaven saw the rainbow, and became joyous[3]. They smiled, and the warmth of their smiles shone down on the earth as sunshine. The warm sunshine made the people on earth happy, and they smiled, too. Now every time it rains, the baby moths, who still have their colors, spread themselves across the sky to make more rainbows.

蛾子为什么是灰色的

蛾子曾经是动物王国中最美丽的动物,他们原本比蝴蝶还要漂亮,他们善良、慷慨、乐于助人。有一天,天使们在天堂里哭泣。她们如此伤心是因为天空乌云密布,她们看不到下面的人们了。天使们的眼泪落下,形成了瓢泼大雨。善良的蛾子不愿意看到大家这么伤心,决定编制一道彩虹。他们想,如果要是请他们的好兄弟蝴蝶们也来帮忙,大家齐心协力,都来贡献一点儿自己的美丽颜色,就一定能编制出漂亮的彩虹。

于是,一只小蛾子飞去向蝴蝶女王求助,可是蝴蝶们都很虚荣和自私,没有一只蝴蝶愿意为天使和人们贡献出自己的一丁点儿颜色。蛾子们只好决定独自编制彩虹,他们拼命扇动和拍打自己的翅膀,五颜六色的粉末集成小小的云朵,风儿将它们匀称地吹展成漂亮的弧线。可惜,弧线太细了。蛾子们继续扇打翅膀,贡献更多的颜色,直到绚烂的彩虹在天空中形成美丽的弧线。除了灰色,他们奉献了所有的颜色,因为灰色不适合这漂亮的彩虹。

现在,原本色彩艳丽的蛾子变得黯淡而灰暗,但天堂的天使看到彩虹却高兴地笑了,她们温暖的笑容普照大地,变成了阳光。暖融融的阳光让地上的人们开心极了,他们也笑了。现在,每当下雨的时候,那些刚降生依旧色彩绚丽的小蛾子们依然飞上天空,去为彩虹添加更多的美丽。

---

[1] moth n. 蛾子

[2] generous adj. 有雅量的,慷慨的

[3] joyous adj. 令人高兴的,欢乐的

Dogs' Friendship

Once, two dogs, Bob and Rover lay outside the kitchen wall, basking[1] in the sunshine. At the gateway of the yard, they might with great pomp have kept their guard, yet as they'd had their fill of meat—and well-behaving dogs by day don't bark at those who pass their way—the pair began to chat, and talked about every mortal thing—the work they had to do, the evil and the good in the world, and last, the friendship too.

Said Rover, "What could fortune happier send than all your life to live with tried and trusted friends, to help each other out if trouble should arise, to sleep, to eat beside your brother, to fight like heroes for each other, to look with fondness in your comrade[2]'s eyes, to see that not one wasted chance went by, to amuse your friend, to make his hour more bright, and in his happiness find all your own delight? Supposing now, for instance, you and I, such bosom friendship was to try! The time would go so fast that we should not see its flight."

"Come on, my boy, all right!" With ardour Bob replied, "Dear Rover, many a time I have felt so mortified that here are we, two dogs, together day and night, yet hardly pass a day without a fight! And why indeed? As our master is so good, we've lots of room and lots of food. Besides, it's quite absurd! Men take us as a type of friendship: tell me then, why friendship between dogs, like friendship between men, is not a thing of which you've heard! Let's show them that between us there is not any bar!"

"Come on, give a paw!" cried Rover, "Here you are!"

And so the newly-made friends at once embraced; each licked the other's face, so glad, they hardly knew with whom to match their case of friendship. "Orestes! Pylades(two good friends in Greek mythology)!" "Brawls, envy, spite, begone!"

Just then, alas! The cook threw out a splendid bone. And look! The newly-made friends were on it like a flash. Accord, friendship melt like wax. Orestes, Pylades, they bit, they tore, they ghashed[3], they filled the air with clumps of hair. What parted the pair at last? Cold water on their backs!

Of friendship such as this the world is full. In fact, it would seem, of friends there's scarce another kind. Describe one pair of them, and all the rest you cover. Hearing them talk, you'd say they had one heart and mind. Then throw them down a bone, and there are dogs all over.

狗的友谊

有一次，两只狗——鲍勃和罗沃躺在厨房外的墙角，暖洋洋地晒着太阳。尽管他们可能会在院子门口威风凛凛地站岗，但是现在，他们已经吃饱了——并且有礼貌的狗是不会在白天对路人狂吼乱叫的——于是，他们开始闲谈起来，谈起人世间的纷纷扰扰——他们不得不做的工作、世间的邪恶与善良，最后，他们也谈到了友谊。

罗沃说："与值得依靠和信赖的朋友终生相伴，共患难、同生死，彼此形影不离，相互嬉闹、关爱，抓住机会投其所好，使朋友快乐开心，在他的幸福快乐中寻找自己的快乐，还有比这更令人愉悦的事吗？比如现在，你我的友情如此深厚，在一起的时间总过得很快。"

"兄弟，你说得很对！"鲍勃热情洋溢地回答，"亲爱的罗沃，许多次，我都感到很苦恼，我们兄弟两个日日夜夜都待在一起，却每天都打得不可开交！真是不知道为什么啊？主人那么善良，我们住得好、吃得饱，而且更可笑的是，人类把我们当作友谊的典范，但为何狗之间的友谊，就像人之间的友谊一样，并非像你听到的那样呢？让我们兄弟俩证明给他们看，我们是亲密无间的！"

"来，握个手吧！"罗沃叫道，"来！"

于是，这两个新结交的朋友立刻相互拥抱，他们舔着对方的脸，兴奋不已，觉得他们才是世界上最好的朋友。"俄瑞斯忒斯！庇拉德斯！（希腊神话中的好朋友）""让吵架、嫉妒和怨恨统统见鬼去吧！"

就在这时，哎，厨师丢出来一根上好的骨头。看啊！两个新结交的朋友立刻扑了上去，什么誓言啊、友情啊，立刻烟消云散。俄瑞斯忒斯！庇拉德斯！他们撕咬着，拉扯着，弄得狗毛满天飞。最后是怎么放开的呢？一桶冷水泼到他们背上！

人世间的这般友谊比比皆是。现实中，天下朋友通常如此，窥一斑便可知全貌。听他们的谈话会让人觉得他们同心同德。而扔一根骨头给他们，就会一下子全变成狗了！

---

[1] bask v. 取暖，晒太阳　　　　　　　[3] gnash v. 咬牙切齿

[2] comrade n. 朋友，伙伴，同志

Fairy[1] Butterfly

There was once a little girl. She had no family, and no one loved her. One day, feeling very sad and lonely, she was walking through a meadow when she noticed a small butterfly caught in a thorn[2] bush. The more the butterfly struggled to free itself, the deeper the thorns cut into its fragile body. The little girl carefully let go the butterfly. Instead of flying away, the little butterfly changed into a beautiful fairy. The little girl rubbed[3] her eyes in disbelief.

"For your wonderful kindness," the butterfly fairy said to the girl, "I will grant you any wish you would like to have."

The little girl thought for a moment and then replied, "I want to be happy!"

The fairy said, "Very good." Then she leaned toward the girl and whispered in her ear. Soon the fairy vanished.

As the little girl grew up, there was no one in the land so happy as she. Everyone asked her the secret of her happiness. She would only smile and answer, "The secret of my happiness is that I listened to a good butterfly fairy when I was a little girl."

When she was very old and in her deathbed, the neighbors all gathered around her, afraid that her secret of happiness would die with her. "Tell us, please," they begged, "tell us what the good fairy said."

The lovely old woman simply smiled and said, "She told me that everyone, no matter how secure they seem, no matter how old or young, no matter how rich or poor, needs me."

---

[1] fairy n. 小仙子, 小精灵　　　[3] rub v. 擦, 搓, 摩擦

[2] thorn n. 刺, 棘

蝴蝶仙子

从前有一个小女孩。她没有家,也没有人爱她。一天,她感到非常难过和孤独,正当穿过一片草地时,她看到一只小蝴蝶被荆棘丛挂住。小蝴蝶越是拼命挣脱,那些刺就越深地插入它那脆弱的身体。小女孩小心翼翼地放开蝴蝶。小蝴蝶没有飞走,而是变成了一个美丽的仙女。小女孩擦着自己的眼睛,感到难以相信。

蝴蝶仙子对小女孩说:"你的心真好,你想许什么愿,我都帮你实现。"

小女孩想了一会儿,回答说:"我想要快乐!"

蝴蝶仙子说:"很好。"然后倾身贴近小女孩,在她的耳边轻声耳语。说完,蝴蝶仙子就突然不见了。

随着小女孩渐渐长大,这块土地上谁也没有像她那样快乐的了。人人都问她快乐的秘诀。她只是微微一笑,回答说:"快乐的秘诀就是我小时候听了一位蝴蝶仙子的话。"

当她老态龙钟临终之际,邻居们都围在她的身边,担心她的快乐秘诀随她一块逝去。他们乞求道:"告诉我们吧,告诉我们蝴蝶仙子都说了些什么。"

这位可爱的老太太只是微微一笑,说:"她告诉我说,每一个人,无论他们多有安全感,无论年纪大小,无论穷富,都需要我。"

Spendthrift and Swallow

A gay young spark I knew, who happened from his aunt of great riches to inherit. He started squandering[1], and squandered with such spirit, that all his worldly wealth became I. O. U[2].

He had a fine fur coat, and new. It was winter at the time. One day a swallow passed in the sky; what does our booby[3] do? He pawned the fur! "Why, aren't we all aware, you'll never see a swallow in the air till spring is in sight! So now," thinks prodigal, "My fur is quite useless. Why wrap oneself in furs? It is now the first spring breeze. To Nature's waking realm[4] brings everything that pleases, and to the silent North the banished Frost takes wing."

Our friend was quick at reckoning. He was only quite forgetful—at least, until he sneezed, one swallow did not make the spring. And so it proved! The frosts returned again. The carts went creaking over the crumbled snow; the chimneys puffed their smoke, on every window pane delightful fairy tracings showed.

Poor rake! His eyes with rheumy moisture flew; the little bird that spoke of spring days to follow, lay frozen in the snow. He stood beside the swallow, trembled, held his breath, and mumbled[5] through his teeth, "You villain, anyhow you're finished too! I thought that I could count on you! Having pawn my fur just now—a bad thing to do!"

---

[1] squander v. 浪费

[2] I. O. U.(I owe you)借据,欠条

[3] booby n. 呆子,傻瓜

[4] realm n. 领域

[5] mumble v. 含糊地说,咕哝着说,抿着嘴嚼

浪子和燕子

　　一个放荡的纨绔少年从他姑妈那里继承了一大笔遗产。他开始大肆挥霍，直到所有的财富都成了欠条。

　　他有一件上好的皮大衣，还是崭新的。当时正值冬季，有一天，天上飞过一只燕子。这个傻瓜做了什么？他把皮衣当掉了！"谁不知道只有到了春天，天空才会出现燕子呢，"浪子想，"所以，现在我的皮大衣没用了，为何还要紧裹着它呢？第一缕春风已经吹过，苏醒的大自然一切都令人心旷神怡，严冬也跑到寂静的北方了。"

　　至少打喷嚏之前，这个少年很会盘算，只是他忘了——燕不成春。确实如此！寒冬又回来了！马车咯吱咯吱地穿过冰天雪地，烟囱冒着烟，窗户玻璃结满了形状各异的冰花。

　　可怜的浪子，泪流不止，而那只代表春天即将到来的燕子冻死在雪地里。浪子站在燕子旁边，冻得发抖，他屏住呼吸，嘴里喃喃道："坏蛋！不管怎么说，你都完蛋了！我以为还能指望你呢！我刚刚把皮衣卖了——简直太糟糕了！"

The Old, Old Wine

Once there lived a rich man who was justly[1] proud of his cellar and the wine therein. And there was one jug of ancient vintage kept for some special occasions known only to himself.

The governor of the state came to visit him, and he bethought him and said, "That jug shall not be opened for a mere governor."

And a bishop[2] of the diocese[3] came to visit him, but he said to himself, "Nay, I will not open that jug. He would not know its value, nor would its aroma[4] reach his nostrils."

The prince of the realm came and dined with him. But he thought, "It is too royal wine for a mere prince."

And even on the day when his own nephew was married, he said to himself, "No, not to these guests shall that jug be brought forth."

Many years passed by, he died. He was buried like every seed and acorn.

And upon the day that he was buried the ancient jug was brought out together with other jugs of wine, and it was shared by the peasants of the neighborhood. But none knew its great age.

To them, all that was poured into a cup was only wine.

188

最 寓言
Zui Fable

---

[1] justly adv. 正当地

[2] bishop n. 主教

[3] diocese n. 主教教区

[4] aroma n. （食物或饮料的）芳香

陈年老酒

从前,有一位富有的人,他很为自己的酒窖和里边存放的美酒感到骄傲。他有一坛陈年老酒,准备在一些特殊的场合享用,这只有他一个人知道。

州长来拜访他,他仔细地想过之后自言自语道:"为一个小小的州长就打开那坛酒不值得。"

辖区的一位主教来拜访他,他自言自语地说:"不,我不会开那坛酒的。他不懂得它的价值,就是酒香扑鼻,他也未必能闻到!"

王子来和他一块吃晚饭,可他想:"这酒太高贵了,一个小王子不配喝啊。"

就是在他的亲侄子结婚的那天,他还是自言自语地说:"不,这酒可不是为那些客人酿制的。"

很多年后,这个老人死了,他像种子和橡子那样被埋入土中。

他下葬那天,那坛陈年老酒和别的酒一起被抱了出来,被周边的农民喝掉了。根本没有人知道它是哪年酿造的。

对他们而言,倒进杯中的不过是酒而已。

The Ass

The day when Jupiter first peopled all the earth, and gave the various tribes[1] of beasts their birth, the ass came somehow into being, too. But whether of intent or having too much to do, the cloud-compeller took no note, so the ass came out no larger than a stoat[2]. Like that, the ass was scarce worth observation, and yet a prouder beast there's not in all creation. The ass was longing to attract all eyes, but being of such a tiny size, he simply felt ashamed to stir. So the conceited ass kept plaguing Jupiter, with prayers that he would make him bigger.

"Why, think!" he complained, "It can't be borne at all, panther, lion, elephant, they each cut such a figure, among the creatures great and small, the talk's eternally of them. And why the ass is so cruelly condemned? That honour lists go by without us, and no one cares to speak about us? If even half the height of calf you'd let me be, I'd stop the lion's pride, the leopard's vanity, and all the world will talk of me."

Next day again, the ass took up the old refrain. And this at last became so tiring. Said Zeus: "Oh, let him have whatever he's desiring. I'll set his mind at ease."

The ass became a portly kind of cattle, besides he got a voice that made so strange a rattle[3]. That now the long-eared Hercules made all the creatures' marrow freeze!

"What beast is that, and from what pack? Sharp teeth, remarkable!"

In fact, the ass was soon one thing talked about. How did it end? It was scarce a year before everyone knew all about the ass. For sheer stupidity his name had come to pass, and all put burdens on his back.

---

[1] tribe n. 部落
[2] stoat n. 白鼬

[3] rattle n. 格格声

驴

朱庇特第一次在地球上造人时,也创造了各类动物,驴也这样诞生了。但是,不知是朱庇特故意所为还是因为太忙没有注意到,驴降生时比白鼬还要小。正是因为如此,驴很少引起人们的注意。然而,他却有其他动物少有的傲气,他渴望得到所有人的关注。但他个头那么小,连活动一下都觉得丢脸。因此高傲的驴不断地乞求朱庇特把他变得大点儿。

"啊,想想吧,"他抱怨道,"这简直无法忍受,豹、狮子、大象,他们每一个都长得那样高大,不管是大动物还是小动物永远都在谈论他们。为什么我们驴就要受到如此残酷的处罚? 荣誉榜上没有我们,谁都不屑谈到我们? 哪怕让我有牛犊的一半身高也行啊,我会让狮子不再高傲,豹也不再虚荣。那样全世界都会谈论我。"

第二天驴子重复前一天的抱怨。宙斯听得不耐烦了,就说道:"哦,就如他所有所愿,让他安静。"

于是驴变成了牲口中的庞然大物,另外,他的声音也变得怪里怪气。这长耳朵的大力士,如今使每个生物都心生恐惧!

"这是什么牲畜啊,属于哪个种族? 他的牙齿尖尖的,真奇怪!"

事实上,驴很快成为谈论的话题。结果怎么样? 几乎不到一年,每个人都对驴很熟悉了。驴因为十足的愚蠢而闻名,于是人们纷纷把重物放在他的背上。

The Travelers and the Bear
旅行者和熊

Two men traveling through a forest together promised to help each other whatever danger threaten[1] them. They had not gone far when a bear rushed[2] at them from the bushes. One man was a good climber, and quickly climbed a nearby tree, but the other, seeing that he had no chance alone against the bear, fell flat[3] on his back, and pretended to be dead. The bear came up to him, sniffed[4] at him, thinking him dead, went off into the woods again without hurting him. When the bear had gone, the other traveler came down from the tree, and smilingly asked his companion what the bear had said to him. "For I could see," he said, "that he put his mouth close to your ear."

"He told me to tell you," replied the other, "that you were a great coward, and that in future I should not trust those who make fine promises, but will not stand by their friends in danger."

两个旅行者一起穿过一片森林,两人都约定无论遇到什么危险,两人都要互相帮助。他们才走了不远,一只熊从灌木丛中朝他们扑过来。他们当中有一个是攀登好手,他很快就爬到旁边的一棵树上,但是另一个人呢,知道他一个人不可能对付得了熊,就直挺挺地仰卧在地上装起死来。熊走到他跟前,嗅了嗅他,以为他死了,没有伤害他,又走进森林里去了。等到熊走远了,另一个旅行者从树上爬了下来,微笑着问他的同伴那只熊对他说了些什么。"因为我看到,"他说,"那只熊把他的嘴凑到了你的耳朵旁。"

"他叫我告诉你,"另一个旅行者答道,"你是一个胆小鬼,将来我再也不应该相信那些只会做出好听的承诺,但遇到危险就丢下朋友不管的人了。"

---

[1] threaten v. 威胁

[2] rushed at 扑向

[3] flat adj. 平的

[4] sniff v. 嗅, 闻

第四章

〰〰〰

生活睿语
Life Sagacity

〰〰〰

The Country Maid and Her Milk Can
村姑和牛奶罐

A country maid was walking along with a can of milk upon her head, when she fell into the following train of reflections. "The money for which I shall sell this milk will enable me to increase my stock of eggs to three hundred. These eggs, allowing for what may prove addle[1], and what may be destroyed by vermin[2], will produce at least two hundred and fifty chickens. The chickens will be fit to carry to market just at the time when poultry is always dear; so that by the New Year I cannot fail to have money enough to purchase a new gown. Green—let me consider—yes, green matches my complexion best, and green it shall be. In this dress I will go to the fair, where all young fellows will strive to have me as a partner; but no—I shall refuse every one of them, with a disdainful[3] toss turn from them."

Contented with this idea, she could not forbear acting with her head the thought that passed in her mind, when down came the can of milk! And all her imaginary[4] happiness vanished in a moment.

一个村姑头上顶着一罐牛奶在路上行走。走着走着,她的脑子里浮现出一连串的幻想:我卖了这罐牛奶后,用这笔钱买鸡蛋,这样我有的鸡蛋可以增加到300个。用这300个鸡蛋孵小鸡,就算有坏的、生虫的,至少也能孵出250只小鸡。等小鸡长大后,正好能赶上卖个好市价,那么到了新年,我就能有钱买一件新礼服。买一件绿色的——让我好好想想——对,绿色与我的肤色最相衬,就买绿色的。我穿上这件衣服去赶集,所有的年轻小伙子都会抢着邀请我做舞伴。但是不行——我要轻蔑地把头一扬,转身过去不理他们,让他们人人都碰个钉子。

她想得得意忘形,情不自禁地把头一扬,刹那间,牛奶罐跌了下来! 她幻想的一切幸福瞬间破灭了。

---

[1] addle adj. 腐坏的

[2] vermin n. 寄生虫,害虫

[3] disdainful adj. 轻视的,傲慢的

[4] imaginary adj. 假想的,虚构的

The Wolf and His Shadow
狼和它的影子

As the sun set to the west, the shadow of any object would become big and long.

There was once a wolf wandering[1] on a plain. Suddenly he discovered that his shadow was very big and long. He started mumbling[2] to himself, "I never thought that I have such a robust[3] body. Since my body is so big, why do I have to be afraid of the lion? Why shouldn't I be called the king of all animals?"

As the wolf thought over this, he grew complacent[4] and arrogant.

He wailed about proudly, wrapped up in his own fantasies. A male lion suddenly pounced on the wolf who was not precautious from the bushes, and pounced him into the ground.

The wolf's dying thoughts were: "How foolish I was! My arrogance has led me to this end!"

夕阳西下,地上所有物体的影子也会随之变得大而长。

一次,一只狼在草原上游荡,突然发现自己的影子竟然是如此的高大,便喃喃自语:"没想到我竟然有这么高大的身躯,既然如此,我为什么还要惧怕狮子呢? 难道我不配担任百兽之王吗?"

狼一心想着自己高大的身躯,变得自满和骄傲起来。

狼骄傲地嚎叫着,沉醉在自己编织的梦境里,突然不远处的丛林中跳出一只雄狮,向这只毫无防备的狼猛扑过来,一下子便把他按倒在地。

临死前,狼悔恨不已地想着:"我是多么的愚蠢啊! 我的妄自尊大是导致我毁灭的原因啊!"

---

[1] wander v. 漫游,闲逛

[2] mumble v. 含糊地说,嘟哝

[3] robust adj. 健壮的,强壮的

[4] complacent adj. 过于自满的,得意洋洋的

The Farmer and His Donkey

One day, a farmer's donkey fell into a dried-up well. The animal cried piteously[1] for hours as the farmer tried to figure out how to save it. Finally, he decided that the animal was old; the well needed to be covered up, and retrieving the donkey just wasn't worth the effort. So he invited his neighbors to come over and help him bury the donkey in the well to put him out of his misery[2].

They all grabbed shovels and began to scoop[3] dirt into the well. At first, the donkey realized what was happening and again cried pitifully. Then, to everyone's amazement, he quieted down. A few shovel loads later, the farmer finally looked down into the well and was astonished at what he saw. With each shovel load of dirt that hit his back, the donkey did something amazing. He shook it off and took a step up!

As the farmer's neighbors continued to shovel dirt on top of the animal, he would shake it off and take a step up. Pretty soon, everyone was amazed as the donkey stepped triumphantly[4] over the edge of the well and trotted[5] off!

---

[1] piteously adv. 可怜地,凄惨地

[2] misery n. 痛苦,不幸

[3] scoop v. 铲

[4] triumphantly adv. 胜利地,得意洋洋地

[5] trot v. （马的）小跑

农夫和驴

一天,一个农夫的一头驴不小心掉进一口枯井里,农夫绞尽脑汁想办法救出驴子,但是几个小时过去了,驴还是在井里痛苦地哀嚎着。最后这位农夫决定放弃,他想这头驴年纪大了,不值得大费周章去把它救出来,不过无论如何,这口井还是得填起来。于是农夫便请来左邻右舍帮忙一起将井里的驴埋了,以免除它的痛苦。

农夫的邻居们拿来铲子,开始将泥土铲进井里。当这头驴意识到自己的处境的时候,又开始痛苦地嚎叫。但是出人意料的是,一会儿之后,驴安静了下来。几铲土下去之后,农夫好奇地探头向井底看去,眼前的情景让他大吃一惊。当铲进井里的泥土落在驴背上时,驴子的反应令人称奇——它将泥土抖落在一旁,然后站到铲进的泥土堆上面!

就这样,驴将大家铲倒他身上的泥土全部抖落到井底,然后站上去。很快地,这头驴便得以上升到井口,然后在众人惊讶的表情中快步地跑开了!

God Is at Work

The only survivor of a shipwreck[1] was washed up on a small, uninhabited island.

He prayed feverishly for God to rescue him out of there, and every day he scanned the horizon[2] to see if any passing-by ships could help him, but none seemed forthcoming.

Exhausted, he eventually managed to build a little hut out of the drift-wood that protected him from the elements, and to store his few possessions.

But then one day, after scavenging for food, he arrived home to find his little hut in flames, the smoke rolling up to the sky.

The worst had happened; everything was lost in that moment. He was stunned[3] with grief and anger. "God, how could you do this to me!"he cried. Instantly, tears came to his eyes.

Early the next day, however, he was awakened by the sound of a ship that was approaching the island. Yes, someone had come to rescue him.

"How did you know I was here?" after boarding the weary man asked of his rescuers.

"We saw your smoke signal." they replied.

---

[1] shipwreck n. 海难   [3] stun v. 使晕倒,使惊吓

[2] horizon n. 地平线

上帝在看着你

在一场海难中，惟一的幸存者随着潮水，漂到了一座无人小岛上。

他天天激动地祈祷上帝能够救他早日离开此地、回到家乡。他还每天注视着海上可否有能够搭救他的过往船只，但是什么也没有。

后来他决定用那片带他来到这个小岛的木头建造一个简陋的小木屋，以保护他在这险恶的环境中生存，并且保存他仅有的财物。

但是有一天当他捕完食物，回到小屋的时候，发现他的小屋竟然陷于熊熊烈火之中，大火引起的浓烟直冲云霄。

最悲惨的是，他所有的一切，都在这一瞬间化为了乌有。他悲痛、气愤地对天大喊："上帝啊！你怎么可以这样对我！"顿时，眼泪从他的眼角流出。

第二天一早，他被一艘正在靠近小岛的船只的鸣笛声吵醒。是的，有人来救他了。

到了船上，他问那些船员："你们怎么知道我在这里?"

"因为我们看到了信号浓烟。"他们答道。

The Lion and the Mouse
狮子和老鼠

The lion was awakened from sleep by a mouse running in front of his face. Rising up in anger, he caught the mouse and was about to kill him, when the mouse piteously[1] entreated, saying: "If you would only spare my life, I would be sure to repay your kindness." The lion laughed and let him go.

It happened shortly after this that the lion was caught by some hunters, who bound him by strong ropes to the ground. The mouse, recognizing his roar, came up, gnawed[2] the rope with his teeth, and set him free, exclaiming: "You ridiculed the idea of my ever being able to help you, not expecting to receive from me any repayment of your favor; but now you know that it is possible for even a mouse to confer benefits on a lion."

一只老鼠从一只狮子面前跑过去,将他从梦中吵醒。狮子生气地跳起来,捉住老鼠,要杀了他。老鼠哀求说:"只要你肯饶恕我,我将来一定会报答你的大恩。"狮子便笑着放了他。

不久之后,狮子被几个猎人捉住,用粗绳捆绑,倒在地上。老鼠听出是狮子的吼声,赶来用牙齿咬断绳索,解救了他,并大声说:"你当时嘲笑我想帮你的忙,而且也不指望我有什么机会报答。但是你现在知道了,就算是小老鼠,也能为狮子效劳的。"

---

[1] piteously adv. 可怜地,凄惨地   [2] gnaw v. 啃,咬

The Secret of Happiness
幸福的秘密

Once there lived a king of endless strength and wealth. Yet, he was not happy. He told his servants[1] to find him things to make him happy, but each came back saying, "Nothing in the world can match the wonderful things you already have." Then in that land, there lived a poor man with a patch[2] over one eye and a crutch[3] to help him walk. Although he had little, he was always happy. When the king heard of this, he asked the man to teach him the secret.

"I never push myself," the man replied, "and I never rush. Most of all, I never wish for too much."

从前有一个国王,虽然拥有绝对的权势和无尽的财富,却并不快乐。他吩咐仆人们四处寻找能使他快乐的东西,但仆人们回来都说:"世界上没有什么东西能比得上您所拥有的一切美好。"当时,那个地方有个穷人,他的一只眼睛上蒙着一块膏药,走路还要拄着拐杖。尽管他身无分文,却总是快乐似神仙。国王听说这件事以后,要这个穷人传授他快乐的秘诀。

"我从不勉强自己,"穷人回答说,"也从不急于求成,尤其是绝不贪多。"

---

[1] servant n. 仆人

[2] patch n. 补丁,膏药

[3] crutch n. 拐杖

The Fox and the Grapes

In a warm sunny morning, a fox was trotting along near a farm happily. He kept an eye out for a bird or a rabbit to catch for his breakfast. Now and then he would sniff the air for signs of danger. He did not want to get caught by the farmers who hated him for always stealing their chickens.

The fox soon passed a vineyard. The thick stems of the grape vines curled[1] round the strong wooden frames and stood tall in the field. From these thick, strong vines, hung huge bunches of purple grapes which looked plump[2] and juicy.

The walk in the sun had made the fox quite thirsty and he looked longingly at the grapes. The fox thought the grapes must be sweet, delicious and juicy.

"I must eat some of those grapes before the farmer comes." he thought.

He walked up to the nearest vine and stood up on his hind[3] legs. He then tried to pluck the lowest bunch of grapes with his teeth. However, the bunch was too high and he could not reach it. He then ran back a few steps and leaped up towards the bunch, opening his mouth wide and trying to snap them with his sharp[4] teeth. He missed!

The fox did not give up easily. For a long time, he kept running and leaping at the bunch of grapes... But no matter how hard he tried, he could not reach the grapes.

In the end, feeling tired, sweated and disappointed, the fox gave up. As he walked away, he muttered, "I don't really need them at all. They are probably sour grapes anyway."

---

[1] curl v.: 盘绕

[2] plump adj. 丰满的

[3] hind adj. 后面的

[4] sharp adj. 锋利的

狐狸和葡萄

一个阳光明媚的早晨，有只狐狸快乐地沿着一条小径走，附近便是农庄。狐狸一边走，一边向四周张望，希望能猎到兔子或鸟做为早餐。狐狸也不时要提防袭击，由于他经常偷吃农夫的鸡，所以他很怕被痛恨他的农夫们捉到。

狐狸经过一个葡萄园。满园的葡萄盘藤而上，高高地在木架上茁壮地生长着。茂密且青葱的葡萄树，悬挂着一大串一大串的葡萄，看起来是那么的水灵和美味。

由于在太阳下走了一段路，狐狸感到非常口渴，看到这些葡萄更令他垂涎三尺。狐狸心想，这些葡萄一定很甜，不但美味，还能解渴。

"在农夫还没发现之前，我一定要弄些葡萄吃。"狐狸想。

于是，他走到最近的葡萄树下，用后肢撑着身体站立起来，然后，他尝试用牙齿去摘最低的一串葡萄。可是，他碰不到那串葡萄。狐狸后退了几步，然后向前一跃，他大张的嘴巴几乎可以咬到葡萄了，可是最终还是扑了个空。

狐狸并没有轻易放弃。他再次后退，再向前冲几步一跃……同样的动作尝试了数十次，仍然没能摘下葡萄。

最后，狐狸疲惫不堪，汗如雨下，心里失望不已。终于，他放弃了！"我才不要吃这些葡萄哩，它们都是酸的！"狐狸自言自语地走开了。

The Cobbler[1] and the Banker

A cobbler passed his time in singing from morning till night; it was wonderful to see, wonderful to hear him; he was more contented in making shoes, than was any of the seven sages. His neighbor, on the contrary, who was rolling in wealth, but little sung, and slept less. He was a banker; when by chance he fell into a doze at day-break, the cobbler awoke him with his song. The banker complained sadly that God had not made sleep a saleable commodity, like edibles[2] or drinkables.

Having at length sent for the songster, he said to him, "How much a year do you earn, Master Gregory?"

"How much a year, sir?" said the merry cobbler laughing, "I never reckon[3] in that way, living as I do from one day to another; somehow I manage to reach the end of the year; each day brings its meal."

"Well then! How much a day do you earn, my friend?"

"Sometimes more, sometimes less; but the worst of it is, and, without that our earnings would be very tolerable, a number of days occur in the year on which we are forbidden to work; and the curate, moreover, is constantly adding some new saint to the list."

The banker laughing at his simplicity, said, "In the future, I shall place you above want. Take these hundred crowns, preserve them carefully, and make use of them in time of need."

The cobbler fancied he beheld all the wealth which the earth had produced in the past century for the use of mankind. Returning home, he buried his money and his happiness at the same time. No more singing; he lost his voice, the moment he acquired that which is the source of so much grief. Sleep quitted his dwelling; and cares, suspicions[4], and false alarms took its place. All day, his eyes wandered in the direction of the treasure; and at night, if some stray cat made a noise, the cat was robbing him. At length the poor man ran to the house of his rich neighbor; "Give me back," said he, "sleep and my voice, and take your hundred crowns."

鞋匠和银行家

一个鞋匠在自己的歌声中度过每一天，无论见到他本人或听到他的歌声都会使人觉得很愉快。制鞋工作对于他来说比当上了希腊七圣还要满足。与此相反，他的邻居是个银行家，拥有万贯家产，却很少唱歌，晚上也睡得不好。他偶尔在黎明时分迷迷糊糊刚入睡，鞋匠的歌声便把他吵醒了。银行家郁郁寡欢地抱怨上帝没有把睡眠也制成一种像食品或饮料那样可以买卖的商品。

后来，银行家就叫人把这位歌手请来，问道："格列戈里师傅，你一年赚多少钱？"

"先生，你问我一年赚多少钱吗？"快乐的鞋匠笑道："我从来不算这笔账，我是一天一天地过日子，总而言之，坚持到年底，每天挣足三餐。"

"好吧，朋友，那么你一天赚多少钱呢？"

"有时多一点，有时少一点；不过最糟糕的是一年中总有些日子不准我们做买卖，否则我们的收入也还算不错。而牧师又常常在圣徒名单上添新名字。"

银行家被鞋匠的直率逗笑了，他说："我要你从今以后不愁没钱用。这一百枚钱币你拿去，小心放好，需要时拿来用吧。"

鞋匠觉得自己好像看到了过去几百年来大地为人类所需而创造出来的全部财富。他回到家中，埋藏好钱币，同时也埋藏了他的欢乐。他不再唱歌了；从他得到这种痛苦的根源那一刻起，他的嗓子就哑了。睡眠离他而去；取而代之的却是担心、怀疑和虚惊。白天，他的眼睛一刻不离地盯着埋藏钱币的方向；夜间，如果有只迷途的猫弄出一点儿声响，他就以为是有人来抢他的钱。最后，这个可怜的鞋匠跑到他那富有的邻居家里说："把你的一百枚钱币拿回去，还我的睡眠和歌声来。"

---

[1] cobbler n. 补鞋匠
[2] edible adj. 可以食用的
[3] reckon v. 设想，估计
[4] suspicions n. 怀疑，疑心

The Crow and the Buffalo[1]

Once upon a time, a farmer had a buffalo whose name was Gejerry. The buffalo got very well with the cow, Gary, the squirrel[2] on the tree and the master's dog. Even the sparrow and the pigeon came to chat with him because he was so friendly to everyone. Buffalo Gejerry was smily to everyone, kind and warm-hearted. But anyhow, he disliked the crow very much.

The crow always flew to the top of pen, where he cawed noisily nearly the whole day. The buffalo felt that it was an unpleasant sound, whereas the voices of the cow, the sparrow, the pigeon and the dog were pleasing and sweet to him. Therefore, whenever the crow came, the buffalo and the other animals all felt unconfortable. The crow was always making noises, or staring at others.

One morning, when the buffalo woke up, he found it hard to open his eyes, as if something was stuck there. He finally could open his eyes but could not see things clearly as if smoething had fallen into his eyes.

The buffalo spoke of his discomfort to the cow Gary. The cow blew a few times into his eyes but with no effect. The buffalo said, "Dear sister Gary, if you were to lick my eyes, it might help a lot."

Instantly, the cow reacted, "Oh, no, my tongue will get infected[3] by that!"

Later on, when the sparrow came hopping to the buffalo, she said, "Good morning, my dear friend, what happened? Why do you have a long face?"

The buffalo appealed to her, "Dear sister sparrow, something has got into my eyes. I feel very uncomfortable. Can you use your beak to peck it out?"

"No!" answered the sparrow. "It will damage my beak." Then she flew away.   Both the squirrel and pigeon also reacted in the same way.

The dog came later. After hearing what the buffalo said, he only grinned and said, "Don't you know that I didn't sleep the whole night? If you don't allow me to sleep now, I will have a backache!"

The buffalo just remained silent after hearing the dog's reply. When he was in trouble, all those whom he considered as friends had refused to help. Tears fell from his eyes and he was very sad indeed.

The crow appeared with his awful cawing as usual. He saw the buffalo with a sad face, and asked, "Oh, dear friend, why are you unhappy?"

Tearfully, the buffalo told him about the unfortunate incident.

"Oh, I see." He flew down from the tree and inspected the buffalo's eyes. He said, "It doesn't matter. There is a tiny bit of hay in your eyes. Let me just pick it out." So saying, the crow gently pulled the hay out from his eyes.

After the hay had been picked out, tears swelled in the buffalo's eyes. His eyes were not in pain anymore and he could see clearly now. His prejudice[4] and dislike towards the crow was washed away by his tears. He learned a lesson from this: when he is successful and happy, everyone could be his friend. But the friend in need is a friend indeed.

From that time onwards, the buffalo became a good friend of the crow. Whenever the buffalo was in trouble, the crow would try his best to help him.

乌鸦和水牛

从前,有个农民养了一头水牛,名叫格杰里。格杰里的脾气很温和,他和同栏的黄牛戈利相处得十分融洽。他跟那些常在院中树上跳来跳去的松鼠以及主人家的狗,也非常有交情。麻雀、鸽子见格杰里这么和蔼可亲,也常常飞来跟他一起谈天说地。总之,水牛格杰里见了谁都是笑眯眯的,显得那么慈祥和热情。可是不知为什么,他对乌鸦特别讨厌。

乌鸦经常飞到牛棚顶上,扯着嗓子"哇哇"地大叫,一叫就是几乎一整天。格杰里觉得乌鸦的声音很难听,对黄牛戈利、麻雀、鸽子、狗等所发出的声音却感觉很悦耳。所以只要乌鸦一来,水牛和其他动物都感到特别厌恶。乌鸦总是在那里喋喋不休,要不就斜着眼睛盯着大家。

这天早上,水牛格杰里一觉醒来,怎么也睁不开眼睛,他的眼睛好像被什么东西粘住了似的。费了好大的劲总算把眼睛睁开了,可是他觉得有什么东西掉进眼睛里,很难受,看东西也模糊不清的。

格杰里把这事告诉黄牛戈利。戈利朝他的眼睛使劲地吹了吹,但是没有什么用处。格杰里对黄牛说:"戈利妹妹,请你用舌头帮我舔一舔眼睛,也许这样我的眼睛就会好起来。"

黄牛戈利一听,赶忙说:"不!那样我的舌头会长疮的!"

不久,麻雀蹦蹦跳跳地来到水牛跟前:"我亲爱的朋友,你早!怎么啦?为什么把脸拉得这样长?"

格杰里央求说:"麻雀小妹妹,不知什么东西掉进了我的眼睛,真难受。请你用嘴巴帮我把那东西啄出来,好吗?"

"不,"麻雀回答说,"这样嘴巴会啄坏的。"说完她拍拍翅膀飞走了。

松鼠和鸽子也都这么回答水牛。

后来,狗来了,他听水牛把事情一说,也皱紧了眉头:"昨天晚上我一夜没睡好,你知不知道?现在你要是再不让我休息,我的腰会累断的!"

一听狗的这些话,水牛格杰里不做声了。平时被当做朋友的伙伴们,到了他有困难的时候，一个也不肯帮忙。他默默地流下了眼泪，感到很伤心。

这时，乌鸦来了，他那"哇哇"的声音仍然是那么难听，乌鸦看见他愁眉苦脸的样子，就问："哎，亲爱的朋友，你为什么不高兴？"

格杰里流着眼泪把自己的不幸遭遇告诉了乌鸦。

"噢，原来是这么回事！"乌鸦说着就从树上飞下来，仔细看了看水牛的眼睛，"不要紧，是一根草掉进了你的眼睛。我马上就把它啄出来！"说完乌鸦就轻轻地把那根草啄了出来。

草一被啄出来，格杰里的眼泪就涌了出来。他的眼睛不痛了，也能清楚地看见东西了。他以前对乌鸦的偏见和恶意也被泪水冲得无影无踪。他明白了一个道理：在自己成功和欢乐的时候，人人都可以成为自己的朋友。然而，只有在患难中伸出友谊之手的伙伴，才是真正的朋友。

从那时候起，乌鸦就成了格杰里的好朋友。无论水牛什么时候有困难，乌鸦总是尽力帮忙。

---

[1] buffalo n. 水牛

[2] squirrel n. 松鼠

[3] infect v. 传染

[4] prejudice n. 偏见

A Heart's–Ease

A story is told of a king who went into his garden one morning, and found everything withered[1] and dying.

He asked the oak[2] that stood near the gate what the trouble was. He found it was sick of life and determined to die because it was not tall and beautiful like the pine. The pine was all out of heart because it could not bear grapes, like the vine. The vine was going to throw its life away because it could not stand erect and have as fine fruit as the peach tree. The geranium[3] was fretting[4] because it was not tall and fragrant[5] like the lilac[6]—and so on all through the garden.

Coming to a heart's-ease, he found its bright face lifted as cheery as ever. "Well, good morning, heart's-ease, I'm glad, amidst all this discouragement, to find one brave little flower. I am gratified that you do not seem to be the least disheartened. Why are you so happy?"

"Yes, I'm very happy, although I don't have much to be proud of, but I don't feel depressed. I thought that if you wanted an oak, or a pine, or a vine, or a peach tree, or a geranium, or a lilac, you would have planted one; but as I knew you wanted a heart's-ease, I am determined to be the best little heart's-case that I can."

They give everything to God without reserve, so they are content with all things; for they only want to be a servant of God, and desire to do for him whatever he desires them to do; they strip themselves of everything, and in this nakedness find all things restored a hundredfold.

---

[1] withered adj. 枯萎了的，凋谢了的

[2] oak n. 橡树

[3] geranium n. 天竺葵

[4] fret v. 发愁，担心

[5] fragrant adj. 有香味的，芬芳的

[6] lilac n. 紫丁香

心安草

一天早晨,国王独自一人在花园中散步,突然发现所有的花草树木都病恹恹的。

国王非常诧异,就问花园门口的一颗橡树,它们究竟遇到了什么麻烦。原来橡树觉得自己不像松树那样高大俊秀,所以消极厌世,不想活了;松树则憎恶自己不能像葡萄藤那样硕果累累;而葡萄藤也想离开人世,因为它终日匍匐在地上,不能挺起胸膛,而且无法像桃树那样结出甜美的果实;天竺葵也病倒了,因为它嫌自己没有紫丁香挺拔、芬芳……就这样,园中所有的花草树木都在自怨自艾。

如今,只剩下一株心安草在那儿一如既往地吐露着芬芳,国王见状很高兴地对它说:"早啊,心安草,当别的花草树木都对自己气馁的时候,只有你还这样勇敢地生活着,真让我感到欣慰啊! 但你为什么能够这样快乐呢?"

"是啊,我很快乐,虽然我身上没有什么值得骄傲的地方但我却从未沮丧过,因为我知道,如果你需要一颗橡树,或是一棵松树,抑或是葡萄藤、桃树、天竺葵、紫丁香的话,你一定会去种植他们;而且我还知道,你只希望我做一株小小的心安草,所以我下定决心做一株最棒的心安草。"

把自己的一切都毫无保留地奉献给上帝,那么他们凡事都会感到满足,因为他们只愿做一个上帝的侍者,只希望能够做好上帝给他们的事。他们如此忠心耿耿,上帝一定会给他们百倍的酬劳。

Mercury and the Woodman

A woodman was felling[1] a tree on the bank of a river, when his axe[2], glancing off the trunk[3], flew out of his hands and fell into the water. As he stood by the water's edge lamenting[4] his loss, Mercury appeared and asked him the reason for his grief. On learning what had happened, out of pity for his distress, Mercury then dived into the river and, bringing up a golden axe, asked him if that was the one he had lost. The woodman replied that it was not, and Mercury then dived a second time, and, bringing up a silver axe, asked if that was his. "No, that is not mine either." said the woodman.

Once more Mercury dived into the river, and brought up the missing axe. The woodman was overjoyed at recovering his property, and thanked his benefactor warmly; and the latter was so pleased with his honesty that he made him a present of the other two axes.

When the woodman told the story to his companions, one of them was filled with envy[5] of his good fortune and determined to try his luck for himself. So he went and began to fell a tree at the edge of the river, and presently contrived[6] to let his axe drop into the water. Mercury appeared as before, and, on learning that his axe had fallen off, he dived and brought up a golden axe, as he had done on the previous occasion. Without waiting to be asked whether it was his or not, the fellow cried, "That's mine, that's mine." and stretched out his hand eagerly for the prize, but Mercury was so disgusted at his dishonesty that he not only declined to give him the golden axe, but also refused to recover for him the one he had let fall into the river.

[1] fell v. 伐木

[2] axe n. 斧子

[3] trunk n. 树干

[4] lament v. 痛惜，感到悲痛

[5] envy n. 羡慕，嫉妒

[6] contrive v. （设法）做成某事，筹划（某事）

墨丘利和樵夫

有一个樵夫在河边砍树，突然，他的斧子飞离了树干，从手中落入了水里。当他站在水边悲叹的时候，墨丘利出现了，问他为什么如此伤心。了解了缘由后，出于对樵夫的同情，墨丘利跳进河里，捞上来一把金光灿灿的斧子，问樵夫这是不是他掉进河里的斧子。樵夫说不是。于是墨丘利第二次跳进河中，又捞起一把银斧子，问是不是他的。"不，那也不是我的。"樵夫答道。

墨丘利再次跳进河里，这次捞上来的正是樵夫掉进河里的那把。樵夫看到失而复得的斧子欣喜若狂，对墨丘利感激万分；而墨丘利也非常赞赏樵夫的诚实，于是就把另外两把斧子作为礼物送给了他。

当樵夫把自己的经历讲述给同伴听的时候，其中一个人对他的好运十分嫉妒，决定也去碰碰运气。于是，他去河边砍树，故意让斧子掉进了河水中。墨丘利像以前那样出现了，知道他的斧子落入水中后，他与上次一样跳进河里捞起一把金斧子。没等墨丘利问他，这个人叫道："这就是我的，就是这个！"并伸手急切地想拿到那把斧子，但墨丘利对他的不诚实十分恼怒，不仅拒绝把金斧子给他，就连他自己落入水中的那把斧子也没有还给他。

The Owl[1]'s Children

A cat was hunting for birds in the forest when he met an owl.

"Dear cat, where are you going?" asked the owl politely.

"I'm going to the forest to hunt for birds." said the cat.

"Oh, Mr. Cat, please do not harm my children."

"What do your children look like? If I can recognize your children, I won't harm them."

"My children are very pretty." the owl said proudly.

"All right, I won't touch the pretty ones!" said the cat.

The cat went around hunting for birds. He jumped from one bush to another, finding several nests, and came to a nest with a few ugly[2] baby birds without any feather.

"They are very ugly-looking indeed!" the cat thought to himself. "These surely cannot be the owl's children." The cat ate them all up.

On his way back home, the cat met the owl again. The owl said, "Oh, dear cat, have you had your meal? Did you harm my children?"

The cat said, "Don't worry, I only ate a few ugly little ones."

When the owl flew back home, she discovered that the cat had eaten all her children, she burst out crying.

---

[1] owl n. 猫头鹰   [2] ugly adj. 丑陋的

猫头鹰的孩子

一只猫到树林里捕鸟,遇见了一只猫头鹰。

"亲爱的猫,你要上哪去呀?"猫头鹰礼貌地打招呼。

"我去林中捕鸟。"猫回答。

"啊,猫先生,你可千万不要伤害我的孩子们。"

"你的孩子长得什么样子? 只要我认得出是你的孩子,就不会吃他们了。"

"我的孩子长得很美丽。"猫头鹰自豪地说。

"我知道了,我不会碰那些美丽的小家伙。"猫回应道。

猫捕鸟去了。他从一丛灌木跳到另一丛灌木,发现了好几个鸟巢。其中一个鸟巢里尽是些有皮无毛的小家伙,丑陋极了。

猫想:"这么丑的鸟,该不会是猫头鹰的孩子吧。"于是猫把他们全吃了。

猫回家的途中,又遇见猫头鹰。猫头鹰问:"亲爱的猫,你吃饱啦? 你没伤害我孩子吧?"

"放心。我只吃了一些很丑的小鸟。"猫说。

猫头鹰飞回巢里,她发现猫已经吃了她所有的孩子,失声痛哭起来。

Give Love Wings

There was once a lonely girl who longed so much for love. One day while she was walking in the woods she found two starving birds. She took them home and put them in a small cage. She cared them with love and the birds grew strong. Every morning they greeted her with a wonderful song. The girl felt great love for the birds.

One day the girl left the door to the cage open. The larger and stronger of the two birds flew out from the cage. The girl was so frightened that it would fly away. As he flew close, she grasped[1] it wildly. She felt glad at her success in capturing it. Suddenly she felt the bird go limp. She opened her hand and stared in horror at the dead bird. Her desperate love had killed it.

She noticed the other bird moving back and forth on the edge of the cage. She could feel its great desire for freedom. It needed to soar into the clear, blue sky. She lifted it from the cage and tossed[2] it softly into the air. The bird circled once, twice, three times.

The girl watched delightedly at the bird's enjoyment. Her heart was no longer concerned with her own loss and gain. She wanted the bird to be happy. Suddenly the bird flew closer and landed softly on her shoulder. It sang the sweetest melody that she had never heard.

[1] grasp v. 抓牢,抓紧   [2] toss v. 扔,抛

将爱放飞

从前,有个寂寞的女孩非常渴望爱。一天,她走在丛林中,发现两只快要饿死的小鸟。她把它们带回家,放入一个小笼子。经她悉心照料,鸟儿一天天强壮起来。每天早晨,鸟儿都要用美妙的歌声向她表示问候。女孩不由得爱上了这两只小鸟。

一天,女孩敞开了鸟笼的小门。那只较大较壮的鸟儿飞出了鸟笼。女孩非常害怕鸟儿会飞走。鸟儿飞近时,她死命将它抓住。她十分高兴,终于又把它捉了回来。突然间,她感觉到鸟儿四肢无力。她张开手,惊恐地盯着手中的死鸟。她不顾一切的爱害死了鸟儿。

她注意到另一只鸟儿在笼边扑闪着翅膀。她可以感觉到它对自由的无限向往。它渴望冲向明净的蓝天。她将它举起,轻轻抛向空中。鸟儿盘旋了一圈,两圈,三圈。

看到鸟儿快乐的样子,女孩很高兴。她的内心不再计较自己的得失。她希望鸟儿幸福。突然,鸟儿飞近了,轻轻落在她的肩上,唱起了她从未听过的最动人的歌。

The Judge and the Thief

There was once a man who lost his pouch[1] and he asked for help from the judge.

"Your Honor," he said, "someone has stolen my pouch. There are many dwellers[2] in my house but I do not know who the guilty one is."

After a while, the judge said, "Call all your housemates here, and I shall find out who the thief is."

Later on, all of them appeared before the judge who said, "Now, I have some magic sticks. Each stick is of the same length[3]. Everyone here will be given one stick. Bring them back to me tomorrow morning. Only the thief's stick will grow longer by a finger's length."

Frightened, the thief tried to think of a way to cover up his theft. Finally he found a solution—he cut the stick shorter by exactly a finger's length.

"When it grows in the night, it will be the same length as the others." he thought, proud of his brilliant plan.

The next morning, when everyone gathered in front of the judge, the length of sticks in their hands remained the same—except the thief's! His was shorter by a finger's length.

The judge pointed at him and declared, "It's you who have stolen the money!" and he was put in jail waiting for the punishment.

---

[1] pouch n. 钱包   [3] length n. 长度，长

[2] dweller n. 居住者，居民

法官和小偷

有一个人,钱包不见了,就跑去找法官。

"法官先生,"他说,"昨晚有人偷了我的钱包。可是家里住着好多房客,我不知道是谁如此卑鄙。"

过了一会儿,法官才说:"叫你家的房客全到这里来,我自有办法指出谁是小偷。"

不久,所有的房客都来到了法官面前。法官对他们说:"现在,我这里有一种神奇的芦苇棍儿,每根都一样长。现在你们每人拿一根,明天早晨再把它们带到我这里。谁要是偷了钱,谁的棍儿就会在夜里长出一指的长度来。"

他们当中的小偷慌了,他开始想,该怎样瞒过法官呢? 想啊想,他终于想出了一个解决的方法——小偷把棍儿撅短了整整一指的长度。

"等它夜里长出来时,就跟其他人的一样长了。"他想,并为他的聪明感到骄傲。

第二天一早,大家都到法官的面前。他们手中的芦苇棍儿都一样长,唯独那小偷的短了一截。

法官指着他大声宣布:"就是你偷了钱!"并下令把小偷关进监狱等候刑罚。

Now and Then

One day, a king was traveling in his own land. He saw a farmer so absorbed in his work that he did not even notice a snake coiling[1] round his leg.

The king shouted, "Dear man, there is a snake on your leg!"

The farmer just shook the snake off and continued his work.

The king was very curious and asked, "Dear man, don't you know that the snake can harm you? You ignored it and kept working. Is the work more important than your life?"

The farmer said, "Your Majesty, the only thing that is threatening me is not the snake but the food. If I don't work hard, when the next spring comes, my family members will starve to death!"

The king sympathized with the farmer, and he instructed[2] his prime minister to give the farmer a big sum of money.

A year later, the king met the farmer again. He was well dressed and looked rather plump. He was not farming now but there was a bandage on his right arm.

The king asked him, "Dear man, how is everyday going? What happened to your arm?"

"Your Majesty," the farmer replied, "my finger was pricked[3] by a thorn on the pumpkin. Now I need a rest to take care of my arm."

The king was astonished[4]. "When you were such a poor man, you were not afraid of a snake bite. You only kept working hard. But now you need a rest after being pricked by a little thorn on the pumpkin!"

The farmer said, "Your Majesty, you have forgotten what people usually say: that was before, now it is different!"

此一时彼一时

有一天,国王正在他的国家里旅游,看见一个农夫正专心地锄地,以至连一条蛇缠住了他的腿都没有发觉。

国王大声惊叫起来:"汉子,你的腿被一条蛇缠住了!"

农夫却毫不在意,抖了抖腿把蛇甩开,依然继续锄地。

国王觉得很奇怪,问:"汉子,你不知道那蛇会咬伤你吗? 你却满不在乎地干活,难道干活比你的命还重要吗?"

农夫说:"陛下,真正威胁我的不是蛇,是食物。如果我不拼命耕作,明年春天我一家老小就会全饿死啦!"

国王听了,很同情这个农夫的困境,他命令首相给了农夫一大笔救济金。

一年后,国王又遇见了那个农夫。他看上去衣着华丽,脑满肠肥,甚为富裕。他没在锄地,右臂缠着绷带。

国王上前问他:"汉子,你现在的生活还好吧? 你的胳膊怎么啦?"

"陛下!"农夫答道,"我的手指被南瓜刺扎了一下,我想歇歇,养养胳膊。"

国王惊叹道:"啊! 想当年你穷的时候不怕被蛇咬死,拼命地干活。现在让南瓜刺扎了一下就想歇息了!"

农夫说:"我尊敬的国王,您忘了此一时,彼一时嘛!"

---

[1] coil v. 盘绕,卷

[2] instruct v. 指示,教导

[3] prick v. 刺痛

[4] astonished adj. 惊讶的

The Crow and the Peacocks[1]

There was once a crow who did not like being a crow for he thought he looked ugly with his plain black feathers. He wished his feathers were as colorful as peacock's feathers.

One day, the crow saw some peacock feathers lying on the ground.

"Oh, this is my lucky day." thought the crow. "With these feathers I can now look as handsome as a peacock."

He quickly picked up the peacock feathers and stuck them in between his own feathers. When he had finished, he went to the lake and looked at his reflection[2]. The crow was pleased with what he saw. In between his black feathers were glossy blue and green feathers.

"Oh, how handsome I look!" the proud and silly crow said to himself. "In fact, I look just like a peacock. Even the peacocks won't recognize me."

Just then, a flock of peacocks came by. They looked very handsome indeed with all their tail feathers spread[3] out like fans. And how proudly they walked up to the lake!

The crow was very happy to see the peacocks. "Aha! Now, I can join the peacocks and be one of them." he thought as he hopped up to them. He tried to spread out his tail feathers like a fan too, but it did not turn out right.

Unfortunately, as soon as the peacocks took one look at him, they knew that the crow was not one of them. They were angry about the crow's dress. "How dare you pretend to be a peacock." they said angrily. "You are only a crow!"

The peacocks attacked the crow in group. They used their sharp beaks[4] to pluck away the peacock feathers. Soon, the crow lost all the peacock feathers that he had stuck on. The peacocks continued attacking the crow.

"Stop! Stop!" cried the crow. "You have taken off all the peacock feathers. Why are you still attacking me?"

"Be quiet!" cried the peacocks. "We are doubting that these black feathers are not yours too!" They carried on pulling out all the crow's own feathers too.

In the end the crow was left without a single feather on his body.

乌鸦与孔雀

有一只乌鸦,向来很不满意自己那身黝黑的羽毛,他认为就是这身羽毛令他看起来丑陋无比。他多希望自己的羽毛能像孔雀的一样美丽啊!

有一天,乌鸦发现地上散落着数根孔雀的羽毛。

"噢!我今天可真是幸运!"乌鸦高兴地想,"如果这些羽毛都贴在我身上,那么我就能像孔雀一样美丽了!"

乌鸦拾起这些孔雀的羽毛,一根一根地塞在自己的羽毛中间。塞好之后,他走到湖边看着自己的倒影,高兴极了!他黑色的羽毛间点缀着华丽的蓝色和绿色羽毛。

骄傲、愚蠢的乌鸦自言自语地说:"啊!我看起来俊俏多了。其实,我现在简直与孔雀没有分别。即使是孔雀也不可能认得出我。"

这时候,来了一群孔雀。他们伸展的尾巴看上去就像一把美丽的大扇子,然后,他们英姿翩翩地向湖边走去。

乌鸦越看越入迷。"啊哈!现在我可以加入到他们的队列中,成为他们的一份子了。"乌鸦边想边走上前去。他尝试将尾巴伸展成一把扇子,然而,尾巴却不听使唤。

不幸的是,孔雀们只看了一眼乌鸦就知道乌鸦不是他们其中的一员。他们看到乌鸦的这身打扮,很是生气,说:"你好大的胆子!竟把自己伪装成一只孔雀。事实上你只是一只乌鸦!"

说着,孔雀们群起攻击乌鸦。他们啄去乌鸦身上的孔雀羽毛。一下子,乌鸦身上的孔雀羽毛全都被拔光了。然而,孔雀们并没有因此而停止,依然继续攻击乌鸦。

"快停下来!"乌鸦叫道,"你们已经拔去我身上的孔雀羽毛了,为何还要攻击我?"

"你给我住嘴!我们怀疑这身黑羽毛也不是属于你的!"说完,孔雀们又继续拔去了乌鸦本身的黑羽毛。

最后,乌鸦身上的羽毛被拔得一根也不剩。

---

[1] peacock n. 孔雀

[2] reflection n. 影像,倒影

[3] spread v. 张开,伸展

[4] beak n. 鸟嘴,喙

The Ostrich[1] in Love

On Sunday the ostrich saw a young lady walking in the park. He fell in love with her at once. He followed behind her at a distance, putting his feet in the very places where she had stepped.

On Monday the ostrich gathered violets[2], as a gift to his beloved. He was too shy to give them to her. He left them at her door and ran away, but there was a great joy in his heart.

On Tuesday the ostrich composed[3] a song for his beloved. He sang it over and over. He thought it was the most beautiful music he had ever heard!

On Wednesday the ostrich watched his beloved dining in a restaurant. He forgot to order supper for himself. He was too happy to be hungry.

On Thursday the ostrich wrote a poem to his beloved. It was the first poem he had ever written, but he did not have the courage to read it to her.

On Friday the ostrich bought a new suit of clothes. He fluffed[4] his feathers, feeling fine and handsome. He hoped that his beloved might notice.

On Saturday the ostrich dreamed that he was waltzing[5] with his beloved in a great ballroom. He held her tightly as they whirled around and around to the music. He awoke feeling wonderfully alive.

On Sunday the ostrich returned to the park. When he saw the young lady walking there, his heart fluttered wildly, but he said to himself, "Alas, it seems that I am much too shy for love. Perhaps another time will come. Yet, surely, this has been a week well spent."

[1] ostrich n. 鸵鸟

[2] violet n. 紫罗兰

[3] compose v. 谱写，写作

[4] fluff v. 抖开，拍松

[5] waltz v./n. 跳华尔兹舞，华尔兹舞

恋爱的鸵鸟

星期天,鸵鸟看到一个年轻的姑娘在公园里散步。他一见钟情,于是就踏着她的足迹远远地一步一步跟在她身后。

星期一,鸵鸟为他心爱的人采摘了紫罗兰作为礼物,可是他过于羞怯没敢送给她,只是把花放在她家门口就跑开了,但心中充满了巨大的喜悦。

星期二,他为心爱的人谱写了一首歌。他反复吟唱,觉得这是他听过的最美妙的音乐。

星期三,鸵鸟在餐厅里看着心爱的人用餐,竟忘了为自己点菜。他高兴得连饿的感觉都没有了。

星期四,他写了一首诗给心爱的人。这是他生平写的第一首诗,可他没有勇气念给她听。

星期五,鸵鸟买了一身新衣服。他抖动羽毛,感觉自己既英俊又优雅,希望能引起心爱的人的注意。

星期六,鸵鸟梦到,在一个豪华的舞厅里,自己和心爱的人跳华尔兹。他紧紧拥抱着她,随着音乐一圈又一圈地旋转。醒来时,他感到精力充沛。

星期天,鸵鸟又来到公园,当他看到年轻姑娘在散步时,心狂跳不止。可他自言自语道:"唉,我在爱情面前太羞怯了,可能还会有下一个机会。不管怎样,这个星期我过得真的很好。"

The Squirrel[1] and the Lion

A squirrel, merrily[2] leaping on the branches of an oak tree, accidentally missed its hole and fell upon a lion that lay at the trunk, basking in the shade. His Majesty awoke in anger, and, raising his shaggy[3] mane, displayed his terrific teeth to the trembling squirrel, who, in the most abject manner, begged forgiveness for the intrusion. "I grant you your life," said the lion, "but on condition that you tell me the reason why you little beings are always so lively and happy, while my time passes so irksomely."

"Yes, sir," replied the squirrel, "I will, in return for your mercy[4], comply with your request; but he who says the truth ought to stand higher than he who hears it; permit me, therefore, to ascend the tree."

The lion consented to this; and when the squirrel was out of his reach he thus addressed him, "You seek to know why I am always merry. Conscience gives me a joyous mind, and learns, sir, that the infallible recipe for happiness—a good conscience—you are in want of. You are day and night oppressed with the sting of iniquity[5] for the crimes and wanton cruelties you have committed. How many animals have you devoured, while I have been employed in carrying nuts to alleviate the distresses of my poor brethren! You hate, but I love! Believe me, there is great meaning and truth in these words, and often I have heard my father observe when young, 'Son, let your happiness be found in virtue, and hilarity will be the constant inmate of your bosom.'"

---

[1] squirrel n. 松鼠

[2] merrily adv. 快乐地,高兴地

[3] shaggy adj. 浓密的

[4] mercy n. 慈悲,宽恕,怜悯

[5] iniquity n. 不正当行为

松鼠和狮子

一只松鼠在橡树枝上欢快地跳来跳去,一不小心从树缝中跌落下来,恰巧落在一头正沉浸在树荫下的狮王身上。狮王醒来大为恼怒,竖起浓密的鬃毛,露出锋利的牙齿,把松鼠吓得不停地颤抖。松鼠胆战心惊地请求狮子饶恕他的冒犯。"我饶了你这条小命,"狮子说,"但有一个条件,你必须告诉我,为什么你们这些小家伙总是生活得很快乐,而我的生活却是如此令人厌倦。"

"好的,陛下。"松鼠回答道,"为了感谢您的宽恕,我会满足您的要求。但是,讲述真理的人应该比听真理的人要站得高一点儿。因此,请您允许我站到树上去。"

狮子答应了。于是松鼠就跳到了狮子够不到的地方,接着说:"您问我为什么总是这么快乐,是道德给了我愉快的心情。陛下您要懂得,拥有快乐的秘诀是要拥有善良的心灵——而您却没有。您整日闷闷不乐是因为您惨无人道、作恶多端。有多少小动物被您无情地吞吃掉了,而我一直忙着运送坚果,来救济我那些可怜的同胞们!您心怀仇恨,而我却心怀友爱!请相信我,我的话里蕴涵着深刻的哲理。在我很小的时候,就常听父亲说,'儿子,你要在美德中寻求快乐,只有这样,快乐才会永远留在你心中。'"

A Wildcat Stealing Chicken
野猫偷鸡

Once upon a time, there was a family living in the mountains. One night, a wildcat sneaked a chicken. When the house-owner discovered the loss and rushed to chase the wildcat, it was already out of sight.

The next day, a trap was set at the spot where the wildcat sneaked in, and a chicken was used as the bait. The family kept vigil through the night. When the wildcat set foot in that place again, he was immediately trussed[1] up by the ropes. The wildcat was tightly[2] bound until he was unable to move any part of his body except the mouth and the legs. And the greedy wildcat was seen struggling to stretch his mouth and legs out to reach the chicken. He kept on inching his way toward the chicken, until his dying breath. His mouth and legs were still in the direction of the chicken after death.

Having seen what happened, the house-owner heaved a regretful sigh and said, "This wildcat would steal the chicken even at the expense of his life. I suppose there are people like this, whose greed for something is so great that they are willing to die for it."

从前,有一家人住在山林里。有一天晚上,一只野猫偷走了一只鸡。主人发觉后赶紧去追,可是野猫已经逃得没有踪影了。

第二天,他和家人在野猫进来的地方装上捕兽的器具,并用一只鸡做诱饵。当晚,他们没有睡觉,彻夜监视着屋外的动静。当野猫又从那个地方进来时,立刻就被绳索捆住了。只见野猫的身子被绳索牢牢地束缚着,只有嘴和腿还可以移动。这时馋嘴的野猫还在拼命地挣扎着把嘴和腿伸向那只鸡。最终用尽了全身的力气,虚脱而死。死时它那嘴和腿还伸向鸡的方向。

这情景,屋主人全都看在眼里。他感慨地叹了一口气,说:"那些为贪财利而死的人,大概也和这只为了偷吃鸡而不要命的野猫一样吧!"

[1] truss v. 捆绑,捆住　　　　[2] tightly adv. 紧紧地

The Brothers in Joint[1] Farming
兄弟合种田

Once upon a time, two brothers were engaged[2] in the farming business.

One year, the siblings[3] decided to join a paddy-growing effort. Every day, the brothers woke up early to work hard in the field and return late. Finally, the harvesting season arrived, all the paddy was ready.

The siblings started to discuss how they would share the crop. The elder brother said, "I'll take the upper part, you can take the lower part."

The younger brother was taken aback as he felt that it was unfair. He protested against such a method of sharing.

Then the elder brother said, "No problem. Next year, you can take the upper part and I'll take the lower part. Wouldn't it be fair?"

The younger one had no choice but to follow what his brother suggested.

The following year, when the younger brother pushed the elder brother to sow the seeds, the latter said, "Let's plant taros[4] this year!"

从前,有一对兄弟,他们以务农为生。

有一年,兄弟俩决定一起合作种稻米。每天兄弟俩起早贪黑,辛勤地在田里干活。终于盼到收获季节,稻谷都成熟了。

兄弟俩开始商量如何分配收成。哥哥对弟弟说:"我拿上半截,你拿下半截。"

弟弟很惊讶,觉得这种分配方法太不公平,便极力反对。

哥哥说:"这不难,等明年,你拿上半截,我拿下半截,那不就行了吗?"

弟弟没办法,只好依了哥哥的意思。

到了第二年,弟弟催哥哥赶快下谷种,哥哥却说:"今年改种芋头吧!"

[1] joint adj. 共享的,共有的

[2] engage v. 从事,雇用(某人)

[3] sibling n. 兄弟,姐妹

[4] taro n. 芋头

The Bird's Beauty Pageant
鸟国选美

All birds gathered and decided to elect[1] the most beautiful bird king.

So, every bird, including the peacock, the egret[2], the oriole[3] and the parrot, took good care of their feathers.

An ostrich also heard about the news. He thought, "I have a bald head and didn't have beautiful feathers. How could I compete with others?"

Then, he came up with an idea. He went to collect the feathers coming off from other birds and put them on himself. Thus, he made himself a very beautiful bird.

As the judge was going to crown him king, suddenly, there was a strong wind. It blew off all the feathers on the ostrich. At that time, all the other birds found that he was a fake.

所有的鸟儿们都聚集在一起决定推选他们当中最漂亮的鸟儿成为他们的国王。

于是,每一只鸟儿,无论是孔雀、白鹭、黄鹂还是鹦鹉,都用心地打理着自己的羽毛。

一只鸵鸟听到了这个消息,想道:"我既没有漂亮的羽毛,而且脑袋还是秃秃的,怎么去跟其他的鸟儿们竞争呢?"

于是他想到了一个办法。他收集了许多其他鸟儿们脱落的羽毛,然后把它们都粘在了自己的身上。就这样,他把自己装扮成了一只漂亮的鸟儿。

正当评委将要为当选国王的鸵鸟加冕时,突然,一阵大风刮过,吹掉了所有粘在鸵鸟身上的所有羽毛。就在那时,鸟儿们发现原来他只是一个冒牌货。

---

[1] elect v. 选举

[2] egret n. 白鹭

[3] oriole n. 黄鹂

The Monkey Who Didn't Fall Down Intentionally[1]
失足跌倒的猴子

A monkey king led a flock of monkeys traveling from hill to hill. They had a lot of fun along the journey. Suddenly, the monkey king stumbled[2] over a stone and fell down to the ground. When the rest of the monkeys saw the king falling down, everyone also fell down on the ground intentionally.

But there was one monkey who stood steadily upright as if nothing had happened.

The monkeys were very angry when they saw that he didn't mimic the king's action. They stood up one after another and went to attack him. They caught and bit him. They scolded him for his arrogance. They said, "You kept standing when the king fell down! Are you trying to show you are superior to the king?"

一群猴子在猴王的带领下，翻山越岭、嬉戏游玩。突然猴王被一块石头绊倒了，摔在了地上。众猴子们见大王摔倒了，便也一只接一只故意绊倒在地上。

但只有一只猴子若无其事地站在那里，一动也不动。

猴子们见他竟然不学大王跌倒的模样，气得咬牙切齿，纷纷从地上爬起来向他发难。他们抓住他、咬他，还破口大骂他傲慢无礼、大逆不道，说什么："大王摔倒了，你却还稳稳地站着，难道你是要显示你比大王还要高人一等吗?"

---

[1] intentionally adv. 故意地　　　　　[2] stumble v. 绊脚，绊倒

The Stingy[1] Rich Man

Once upon a time, there was a very stingy rich man. He had been sick for a very long time, and he knew that his days were numbered[2]. One day, he called all his family members to his bedside and said, "I have donated[3] a huge sum of money to repair and renovate[4] the temple, yet God has not shown me any mercy. Remember, after I pass away, do not spend any more money on this cause!"

His family replied, "Yes, how about the funeral procession—do we need to use a coach?"

"No, if you use a coach, you will have to pay the coachman!"

"Then, could we use a wagon[5]?"

"You will have to pay the owner too!"

"We just ask two persons to carry then!"

"No, no, you need to pay them too!"

"What shall we do then?" the family didn't know what to do.

"Oh dear, that is so troublesome. I think I'll just go by myself after death!"

---

[1] stingy adj. 吝啬的，小气的

[2] numbered adj. 有限的，日子不多的

[3] donate v. 捐赠，赠送

[4] renovate v. 修复，翻新

[5] wagon n. 四轮运货车

吝啬鬼

从前,有一个非常吝啬的富人,病了很久,自己也知道命不久矣,有一天就把全家人叫到病床前,对他们说:"以前修建寺庙的时候,我捐过许多钱,可是直到现在,极乐世界什么好处也没给过我,我死了以后,你们别在这方面再花钱了,记住了吗?"

家人回答说:"记住了。那么,出殡的仪式呢? 用不用轿子来抬?"

"不,用轿子的话,就得付钱给抬轿子的人。"

"那么,租辆马车吧?"

"那也得付租车的钱啊!"

"那……还是叫两个人扛吧?"

"不,不,那还得花钱雇两个人来扛。"

"那究竟该怎么办呢?"家人一筹莫展地问。

"唉,真麻烦! 我死了以后,还是自己走路去吧!"

The Kitten Who Went Fishing

One day, a kitten and a big cat went fishing together.

When the kitten saw a flying dragonfly[1], she put the fishing rod[2] aside and went chasing it. She was empty-handed when she came back, but the big cat had caught a big fish.

After a while, the kitten saw a butterfly[3] wandering arround the nearby flowers. Again, she threw down the fishing rod and went to chase the butterfly. The butterfly flew away and the kitten came back to the riverbank empty-handed again. Meanwhile, the big cat had caught another big fish.

The kitten said anxiously[4], "It's so weird. Why do the fish never come to my rod?"

The big cat took a look at her and said patiently, "If you want to fish, make sure that you concentrate[5] on it. Don't go chasing after the dragonfly or the butterfly. If you do that, how do you expect to get the fish?"

The kitten took the big cat's advice and concentrated on her fishing. She did not bother with the dragonfly, or the butterfly. After a short while she caught a big and fat fish too, and she smiled very happily.

---

[1] dragonfly n. 蜻蜓

[2] rod n. 杆，竿

[3] butterfly n. 蝴蝶

[4] anxiously adv. 忧虑地，不安地

[5] concentrate v. 集中

小猫钓鱼

一天,小猫和大猫一起到河边去钓鱼。

正在钓鱼的时候,小猫看见了一只蜻蜓,在空中飞来飞去,她立刻扔下钓鱼竿去追蜻蜓。最后小猫空着手回到垂钓的地点来。这时的大猫已经钓到了一条大鱼。

过了一会儿,小猫又看见了一只蝴蝶,在附近的花丛中徘徊着,她又马上扔下钓鱼竿去追。结果蝴蝶扑扑翅膀也飞走了,小猫又空着手回到河边,这时的大猫又钓上了一条大鱼。

小猫非常着急地说道:"真奇怪,鱼儿为什么总不上我的钩呢?"

大猫看了小猫一眼,耐心地说:"你想钓鱼呀,必须集中精神。一会儿追蜻蜓,一会儿追蝴蝶的,怎么能钓上大鱼呢?"

小猫听了大猫的话,把注意力都集中在钓鱼这件事上,什么蜻蜓啊,蝴蝶啊,她都不看一眼,果然没多久,一条又肥又大的鱼儿上了小猫的钩,小猫笑得合不拢嘴。

The Roar of the Mountain

Once upon a time, there was a big and beautiful mountain in a remote[1] village. The mountain was covered with trees which lived for centuries and provided shade to the villagers. Its surroundings were tranquil[2] with occasional sounds of running water, rattling leaves and the cry of the peddlers[3]. The villagers lived a simple yet carefree life.

One day, the mountain suddenly shuddered. A roaring sound was heard from afar. It plunged the village into chaos. Many people put their work aside and gathered around to find out what happened.

Then another roaring sound was heard from the mountain when the villagers were discussing. This time it was more deafening. Some men predicted the coming of an earthquake. The women argued that there was a giant struggling to free himself from the cave.

The mountain kept on roaring, and people from miles away waited anxiously and feared some possible disaster. Suddenly a little mouse ran out of the cave. At the sight of the large audience[4], it fled in panic into the shrubs[5].

The mountain was silent now, but the people still stood there. After some time of silence, the crowd dispersed and people went home one by one.

The roar of the mountain in the morning remained a mystery to the whole village. Nobody realized that it was only an echo created by a little cave mouse!

最
寓言 Zui Fable

---

[1] remote adj. 偏远的

[2] tranquil adj. 平静的，宁静的

[3] peddler n. 小贩

[4] audience n. 观众，听众

[5] shrub n. 矮树，灌木；甜酒

大山的吼叫

很久以前,在一个遥远的乡下,有一座高大美丽的山。山上都是树林。过去数百年来,这座山一直都供村民遮荫,周围一片宁静。在这里能听到山林间传来的淙淙流水声、树叶被大风吹动的声音,还有小贩叫卖的声音。村民的生活简单而自在。

有一天,这座山忽然受了大震动,远处传来了轰鸣声,这声音使村子陷入了混乱。许多人放下手中的工作从四面八方跑来,纷纷讨论着到底发生了什么事情!

在人们议论纷纷的时候,山再次发出呻吟声,比之前那一次声更大。一些男人猜测是地震的预兆;一些女人则猜测有个巨人困在山洞里,挣扎着要出来。

山一次又一次地呻吟,数里以外的人们都来观看。正当人们屏着气息等着看有什么可怕灾难发生时,一只小老鼠突然从山洞里跑了出来。它一看见人潮,就吓得逃到草丛里去了!

人们仍然站在那里,可是山已安静下来了。等了好久,依然没有什么动静,人潮也就逐渐散去,一个个回家去了。

到最后整个村庄没有人知道山为何要捉弄他们一个早上;也没有人知道山的声音只不过是一只小老鼠在山洞里所发出的回声!

The Miser

Once upon a time, there was a miser who was interested in nothing except money. He sold everything in his house and bought a bar of gold. He stared[1] at the gold and said, "This is the most wonderful thing I have ever dreamed of!"

The miser started to worry that someone might steal his gold. Then he felt that burying[2] the gold deeply under the earth might not be a bad idea after all.

He buried it and dug it out every day to enjoy looking at it for a while. Then he covered it up again in the pit. He felt assured only when he saw the gold was still there.

Soon his weird behaviour was noticed by the neighbor. One night, when the miser was away from home, the neighbor dug into the site and removed the bar of gold.

The next morning, when the miser went into his garden to check on his treasure as usual, he found only an empty pit. The miser could not help but cry his heart out. Another neighbor came to console[3] him. When he was told the whole story, he gave the miser some advice, "Why don't you just simply bury a stone under the ground? After all, you just stare at it without using it. So what's the difference between a stone and a gold bar?"

---

[1] stare v. 凝视，盯着看　　　　　　　[3] console v. 安慰，慰问，抚慰
[2] bury v. 埋藏，掩埋

守财奴

　　从前,有个守财奴,除了金钱,世上任何东西都引不起他的兴趣。他把家里所有的东西都卖掉,换了一块金子,他盯着金子说:"这才是我心目中最美好的东西!"

　　他开始担心这块金子被别人偷走,整天坐立不安。后来他想到一个不错的办法。他把这块金子深深地埋在泥土里。

　　每天,他都把金子挖出来好好欣赏一番,然后再将它埋回去。只有看到金子还在里面,他才放心。

　　渐渐地,他的怪异行为被邻居发觉了。一天趁守财奴不在家时,那邻居拿了铲子去挖掘那儿的泥土,果然,从泥土里挖出一块金子。

　　第二天早晨,守财奴跟平常一样到花园里去观看他的宝物,可是看见的只有空无一物的大坑。守财奴不禁抱头痛哭。另一个邻人过来安慰他,问明缘故后,便说:"那还不简单,你只要把一块石头埋进土里,把它当作金子看待不就行了?反正你只是看金子,又不用它,那么金子跟石头又有什么分别呢?"

Two Peasants[1]

After the French had left Moscow, two peasants went out to search for treasures. One was wise, the other stupid. They went together to the burnt part of the city, and found some scorched[2] wool. They said, "That will be useful at home."

They gathered up as much as they could carry, and went home with it. On the way they saw lying in the street a lot of cloth. The wise peasant threw down the wool, seized as much of the cloth as he could carry, and put it on his shoulders. The stupid one said, "Why throw away the wool? It is nicely tied up, and nicely fastened on." And so he did not take any of the cloth.

They went farther, and saw lying in the street some ready-made clothes that had been thrown away. The wise peasant unloaded the cloth, picked up the clothes, and put them on his shoulders, but the stupid one said, "Why should I throw away the wool? It is nicely tied up and securely fastened on my back."

They went on their way, and saw silver plates scattered[3] about. The wise peasant threw down the clothes, and gathered up as many silver plates as he could, and started off with it; but the stupid one did not give up his wool, because it was nicely tied up and securely tied on.

Going still farther, they saw gold lying on the road. The wise peasant threw down his silver and picked up the gold; but the stupid one said, "What is the good of taking off the wool? It is nicely tied up and securely fastened to my back."

And they went home. On the way a rain set in, and the wool became water-soaked, so that the stupid man had to throw it away, and thus reached home empty-handed; but the wise peasant kept his gold and became rich.

两个农夫

　　法国人撤离莫斯科后,两个农夫出来寻找值钱的东西。他们当中一个聪明,一个愚蠢。两人结伴来到城里被烧毁的地区,发现了一些已烧焦的羊毛,都说:"这些羊毛在家里总会派上用场的。"

　　他们尽自己所能,收集了足够的羊毛,然后背起来返程回家。在路上,他们看见许多布匹被扔在街上,于是,聪明的农夫扔掉羊毛,背上自己能扛下的所有布匹。而那个愚蠢的农夫却说:"为什么要丢掉羊毛呢?我已经把它们捆得牢牢的,扎得紧紧的了。"所以他一点儿布匹都没拿。

　　他们继续赶路,又看到街上扔了一些成衣。聪明的农夫放下布匹,捡起成衣,扛到肩上。愚蠢的农夫说:"我为什么要丢掉这些羊毛呢?我把它们捆得牢牢的,扎得紧紧的,都扛在背上了。"

　　他们接着赶路,又看见了一些散落的银质餐具。聪明的农去将成衣丢掉,然后收集了尽可能多的银质餐具带走了;但愚蠢的农夫仍不肯丢弃他的羊毛,因为它们已经捆得牢牢的,扎得紧紧的了。

　　又走远一些,他们看见路上有金子。聪明的农夫扔掉银质餐具,捡起了金子。但愚蠢的农夫仍然说:"将羊毛拿下来又有什么好处呢?它们毕竟都已经捆得牢牢的,扎得紧紧的,都在我背上了。"

　　于是,他们往家走。半路上下起了雨。把那些羊毛淋了个透湿,愚蠢的农夫只好将它们全都丢掉,两手空空地回了家;而聪明的农夫却因为那些金子而变得富有起来。

---

[1] peasant n. 农民,农夫

[2] scorch v. 烧焦,烤焦

[3] scattered adj. 散乱的,散布的

Jupiter and the Sheep

The sheep was once forced to submit[1] too much harm from other animals. He therefore appeared before Jupiter, and begged him to lessen[2] his misery. Jupiter agreed, and said to the sheep, "I see plainly, my pious creature, that I have created you too defenseless. Now choose what I have best to remedy this fault. Shall I arm your jaws with terrible fangs[3] and your feet with claws?"

"Oh, no!" exclaimed the sheep, "I will have nothing in common with the beasts of prey."

"Or," said Jupiter, "shall I make your bite poisonous?"

"Alas!" replied the sheep, "The poisonous snakes are so sadly detested."

"Well, what shall I do? Shall I plant horns on your forehead, and give strength to your neck?"

"Nor that, gracious father; I should then butt like the goat."

"At the same time you would be able to injure others, if I gave you the means of defending yourself."

"Should I indeed?" sighed the sheep, "Oh! Then leave me, merciful father, as I am. For the power of injuring would, I am fearful, awake the desire of doing so; and it is better to suffer harm, than to inflict[4] it."

Jupiter blessed the pious sheep, who ceased from that moment of his complaint.

---

[1] submit v. 听从，服从

[2] lessen v. 减少，减轻

[3] fang n. 长而尖的牙

[4] inflict v. 使遭受

朱庇特和绵羊

从前，绵羊深受其他动物的伤害，因此，他来到神王朱庇特面前，恳求朱庇特减少他的苦难。朱庇特答应了他的请求，并对他说："我很清楚，虔诚的小东西，我的确没有赋予你太多自我保护的能力。现在你可以选择一种最好的方法来让我弥补这一过失。是给你装上尖牙，还是给你的脚装上利爪呢？"

"啊，不要！"绵羊叫道，"我不希望和猛兽有什么共同之处。"

"或者，"朱庇特又道，"帮你把牙齿灌入毒汁，怎么样？"

"唉呀！"绵羊回答，"毒蛇是最让人痛恨的。"

"那该怎么办呢！要不给你的额头装两只尖角，让你的脖子更加有力，可以吗？"

"神王啊，这也不好，那样我就会像山羊一样顶撞其他动物了。"

"我给你自卫武器的同时，你也就拥有了伤害其他动物的能力。"

"真的会那样吗？"绵羊叹息道，"唉，仁慈的神王啊，那你还是让我保持原样吧。因为如果我拥有了伤害其他生命的能力，我担心，那会引起我伤害其他生命的念头。与其伤害别人，还是自己受点儿苦好。"

朱庇特为虔诚的绵羊祈祷祝福。此后，绵羊也不再抱怨了。

The Olive[1] Tree and the Fig[2] Tree

The olive tree and the fig tree were talking one winter day.

"I feel sorry for you," said the olive tree, "Every winter you lose all your leaves and have to shiver through the winter with bare branches. But I stay green and beautiful all the year round. Still, I suppose we can't all be good-looking."

The fig tree was silent. Later that day the weather turned very cold. Great grey clouds filled the sky and it was very quiet. It began to snow heavily.

All that night it snowed, and all the next day. Fields and hedges were thickly covered and people had to dig paths from their houses to the roadside. The snow settled on the olive tree, drifting in little piles on the leaves, weighing down the branches so that they snapped and fell to the white ground below. The fig tree was more fortunate. She had no leaves to trap the snow and it drifted harmlessly through the bare twigs.

When the thaw[3] came the Fig tree was still standing, ready to put out her new spring leaves; but the olive tree lay broken, a twisted jumble of sticks and brown leaves.

最
寓言
Zui Fable

---

[1] olive n. 橄榄

[2] fig n. 无花果树

[3] thaw n. (冰雪等)融化

橄榄树和无花果树

一个冬日,橄榄树和无花果树聊起天来。

"你真可怜,"橄榄树说,"每年冬天,你的叶子都会掉光,只剩下光秃秃的树枝,在寒冬中瑟瑟发抖。可我一年四季都郁郁葱葱、漂漂亮亮。当然了,世界上总有美丑之分的。"

无花果树沉默无语。那天晚些时候,天变得很冷。天空布满了大片乌云,万籁俱寂,开始下大雪了。

雪整整下了一个晚上,第二天又下了一整天。田野和树篱都覆盖了一层厚厚的雪,人们只好从家门口挖出一条条小路通往路边。雪花落在橄榄树上,一点点地堆积在叶片上。树枝被压弯了,最后折断了,掉落在白皑皑的雪地上。无花果树比较幸运,她没有叶子,挡不住雪,雪从光秃秃的嫩枝间飘过,丝毫没有损害到树。

积雪融化了,无花果树依然挺立,准备一到春天,就吐露新芽,长出嫩叶;而橄榄树却被压断了,成为一堆乱糟糟的残枝败叶。

How Poor We Really Are

One day a wealthy father took his son on a trip to the country-side so he could have his son see how poor country people were.

They stayed one day and one night in the farmhouse of a very humble farm. On the way back home at the end of the trip the father asked the son, "What do you think of the trip?"

The son replied, "Very nice, Dad."

The father then asked, "Did you notice how poor they were?"

The son replied, "Yes, I guess so."

The father then added, "And what did you learn?"

About this question, the son thought for a moment and answered slowly, "I learned that we have one dog in the house but they have four. We have a fountain in the garden but they have a stream that has no end."

"We have fancy lanterns in our garden, while they have numeral shining stars. Our garden goes to the edge of our yard, but for their back yard they have the entire horizon[1]!"

At the end of the son's reply, the rich father was speechless[2]. His son then added: "Thanks, Dad, for showing me how poor we really are."

---

[1] horizon n. 地平线   [2] speechless adj. 说不出话来的

我们是多么贫穷

一天，一个富有的爸爸带着儿子做了一次乡村之旅，他想让儿子明白乡下人是多么的贫穷。

他们在一个农家的寒酸的农场上待了一天一夜。在旅程结束回家的路上，爸爸问儿子："你觉得这次旅行怎么样？"

儿子回答："非常好，爸爸。"

爸爸接着问："你有没有注意到他们是多么贫穷啊？"

儿子答道："是的，或许是吧。"

爸爸追问道："那你都学到了些什么？"

关于这一问题，儿子想了一会儿，慢条斯理地回答道："我学到我们家只有一只狗，而他们却有四只。我们花园里有一个喷水池，而他们却有一条没有尽头的小河。"

"我们花园里有色彩夺目的灯笼，而他们却有无数闪亮的星星。我们院子的尽头就是花园，而他们的后院却有开阔的视野。"

儿子说完后，这个富有的爸爸无言以对。儿子还说道："谢谢你，爸爸，让我明白了我们是多么贫穷。"

The Kind Fox

One day, a careless man shot down a robin[1].

If all the harm had stopped at that! But it did not. Alas! The fatal blow set three small hearts throbbing; her three poor helpless chicks were orphaned by that shot. These chicks have just been hatched; little wit and little strength they've got. They miss their supper-giver; with cold they shiver. They call their mother back with plaintive little squeaks[2].

"Who would not be distressed these piteous[3] babies to see? Whose heart will not grow warm with sympathy?" So to the birds Dame Foxy said, half squatting on a stone just underneath their nest:

"Kind friends, you won't desert these children in their need. Let each for the poor chicks to bring some offering strive! Let each into their nest his wisp of straw contrive[4]! By this you'll keep these babies alive. What's better than a kindly deed?

"Come, cuckoo, use your wits! You're moulting[5], and it is plain. Now isn't it more useful to pluck yourself instead, and with your feathers make a downy little bed? You'll lose them anyhow, to no one's gain."

"You, lark—enough of taking headers, and doing circles in the air! You should be seeking food about the fields and meadows, to give these orphaned babies a share."

"You, woodpigeon—your chicks by now their wings have spread. I'm sure they're old enough to earn their daily bread; why can't you quit your nest on yonder tree? To these poor chicks a mother you could be. Of your small pigeons over there, let God take care!"

"You, swallow, catch some flies for them to eat! Poor orphaned mites, they need a treat!"

"And you, my nice, kind nightingale, you know how all are delight when you are nigh; while zephyrs[6] gently sway their little nest so frail, do send them off to sleep with your sweet lullaby[7]!"

"Such care and tenderness, I feel assured, might make them even forget the loss of mother they have endured. Do what I ask! Let's show what kind heart there is even in the wild. Let's show..."

She'd hardly got so far, when all those three tiny robins could hold no more, for hunger, to the tree, and came tumbling down at Fox's side. And Fox—she dropped her sentiments so fine, and sat straight down to dine.

善良的狐狸

一天,有人无意中射下了一只知更鸟。

如果,只有这点灾难也就罢了,然而还不止这些。哎!这一枪把三只可怜的小知更鸟变成了无依无靠的孤儿。他们是刚孵出来的,什么都不知道,也没有什么力气。他们想念给他们喂食的妈妈,又冻得瑟瑟发抖,哀伤地小声呼唤着母亲回来。

"看到这些可怜的娃娃,谁不觉得心疼,谁不满怀深切的同情呢?"狐狸半蹲在知更鸟巢下面的一块石头上,对其他的鸟儿说道:

"仁慈的朋友们,你们可不要冷眼漠视这些身处绝境的小鸟们啊!为了这些可怜的小鸟,我们大家都出一份力吧!大家想办法搞点儿稻草铺在他们的鸟巢里!这样这些娃娃们才能活下去,难道还有比友善之举更好的事吗?"

"来吧,杜鹃,用用你的脑筋吧!很明显,现在你在换毛,与其让它白白脱落,不如把它们拔下来做一张柔软的小床,反正它们早晚要掉,且毫无用处。"

"你,云雀,你在空中绕圈儿翻筋斗,也玩够了吧!你应该到田野和草原上去寻找食物,分一份给这些孤儿们。"

"你,斑鸠——你的小斑鸠已经羽翼丰满了,我想他们已经长大了,可以自己觅食了。为什么你不离开自己的老窝? 到那边去给三只小鸟当母亲吧。这边你自己的小斑鸠,自会有老天爷照顾的!"

"你,燕子,捉几只苍蝇给他们吃吧,可怜的小孤儿们,需要好好照顾呢。"

"还有你,我美丽善良的夜莺,你知道大家都会因为你的陪伴而感到非常高兴。当他们脆弱的小巢在微风中轻轻摇晃时,你一定要用甜蜜的催眠曲,让他们美美地睡觉。"

"我想如此细心地呵护,一定可以使他们忘记失去母亲的痛苦。按照我的话去做吧!即使是在荒野里,我们也要展现出自己的仁慈,展现出……"

狐狸还在大放厥词,那三只小知更鸟已经饿昏了头,支持不住地从树上栽了下来,正好掉在狐狸身旁。那狐狸——把高尚的情操忘得一干二净,立刻坐下来享用美餐了。

[1] robin n. 知更鸟

[2] squeak n. 尖叫声;吱吱声

[3] piteous adj. 哀怨的;可怜的

[4] contrive v. 发明;设计;图谋

[5] moult v. 脱毛;换毛

[6] zephyr n. 西风,(凉)和风,徐风

[7] lullaby n. 催眠曲;摇篮曲

The Frog and the Bullock
蛤蟆和牡牛

A frog watched a bullock grazing near and resolved that she'd try her best to match his girth[1] and height; she was an envious frog. See how she puffed[2] and swelt and strained with all her might.

"Come, tell me, dear, am I as big as him?" she asks a friend.

"Oh no, my dear. Not nearly."

"Now just you watch me stretch! Look close, and tell me clearly. Well, then! You see? I'm filling out?"

"It doesn't seem much different to me."

"Well—now?"

"Just like you were at first."

At last her wild attempts passed the bounds of nature; she never swelled[3] to bullock's size, but she strained so hard that she cracked and burst.

一只蛤蟆看见一头牡牛正在附近吃草,就想尽全力与他比试腰围和身高;她是一只嫉妒心很强的蛤蟆。瞧,她正用尽全力喘息,挺肚皮呢。

"你看,亲爱的,告诉我,我是不是和牡牛一样大了?"她问朋友。

"噢,没那么大,亲爱的,还差得远呢。"

"你再瞧瞧,现在我鼓得更大了,看仔细点儿,跟我说清楚。嘿,你看,怎么样?我越来越大了吧?"

"看起来和刚才没什么区别啊。"

"呃——那现在呢?"

"还是和你原来一样。"

最后,蛤蟆狂妄的行为超过了她的限度,她的肚皮永远不可能膨胀到牡牛那般大小,由于用力过猛,肚皮爆破了。

---

[1] girth n. 周长,腰身

[2] puff v. 喘息,膨胀

[3] swell v.（使）膨胀,扩大

The Fox and the Tiger
狐狸和老虎

An Archer, hunting in the woods, was so successful with his arrows[1] that he killed many of the wild animals. This frightened the rest so much that they ran into the densest[2] part of the bushes to hide. At last, the Tiger stood up, pretending to be very brave, and told the other animals not to be afraid anymore, but to rely on his courage, and he would attack the enemy on his own. While he was talking, and lashing his tail and tearing at the ground with his claws to impress the others, an arrow came and pierced his ribs. Instantly the Tiger howled with pain.

While he was trying to draw out the arrow with his teeth, the Fox went up to him and asked, in surprise, "Whoever had the strength and courage to wound such a brave and mighty beast as the Tiger?"

"Nay," said the Tiger, "I misjudged my enemy. It was that unbeatable man over there who defeated me!"

一个射手正在森林里打猎。他的箭法好极了,射死了许多野兽。这可吓坏了余下的动物,他们都跑到最茂盛的灌木丛中躲藏起来。最后,老虎站了起来,装着非常勇敢的样子叫其余的动物不必再害怕。凭借他的勇气,他将独自向敌人进攻。他一边说着,一边甩动着他的尾巴,并用他的爪子刨着地上的泥土,想使别人更信任他。就在这时,一枝箭飞来,刺穿了他的肋骨,老虎顿时痛得吼叫起来。

正当他尽力用牙齿拔出身上的箭时,狐狸走上前来吃惊地问道:"谁能有这样的力气和胆量来伤害像老虎这样勇敢而强有力的野兽呢?"

"不,"老虎说,"我错误地判断了我的敌人,是那个不可战胜的人打败了我。"

---

[1] arrow n.箭　　　　　　　　[2] dense adj. 密集的,浓厚的

Values
价值

Once a man unearthed[1] in his field a marble[2] statue of great beauty. And he took it to a collector, who loved all beautiful things, and offered it to him for sale. After the collector bought it for a large price. And they parted.

And as the man walked home with his money, he thought, and he said to himself, "How much wealth this money means! How can anyone give all this for a stone buried and undreamed of in the earth for thousands of years?"

Now the collector was looking at his statue, thinking, and he said to himself, "What beauty! What life! The dream of what a soul!—And fresh with the sweet sleep of a thousand years. How can anyone give all this for money, dead and dreamless?"

　　从前，一个人从他的田地里挖出了一尊精美绝伦的大理石雕像。于是，他把它带到一个喜爱珍藏世界精品的收藏家那里，打算卖给他。这位收藏家以高价买下了它，交易完成后，两人就道别了。

　　这个人拿着钱走在回家的路上，暗自思量："这笔钱意味着多少荣华富贵啊！怎么会有人以此换取一块在地下埋了数千年、做梦都想不到的石头呢？"

　　就在同时，收藏家端详着雕像，凝思着自言自语道："多么精美，多么生动啊！梦幻中的精灵！——沉睡了一千年之后再次恢复生机！竟有人以此珍品换取那些既呆板又俗气的铜臭？"

[1] unearth v. 发掘，掘出（某物）　　　[2] marble n. 大理石

Leave Time Behind You
把时间放在身后

An old monk[1] often took a young monk to the hill outside the temple to read the lection.

One day the young monk said to the old monk, "How slowly the time goes!"

The old monk said, "You can have a try like this—in the morning sit to the west to read, and in the afternoon sit to the east to read."

At the master's advice, the young monk recited the lection against the sun. By and by he neglected[2] the passage of time.

The next day he told the old monk, "Master, you are so great that I forget time in the switch of direction and absorb myself in the lection."

The old monk said, "Whatever you do, only when you leave time behind, you can focus on it selflessly."

老和尚经常带着小和尚到寺院外面的山上诵读经文。

有一天,小和尚对老和尚说:"时间过得真慢呀!"

老和尚说:"你这样试试——上午,你面朝西边坐着读;下午,你面朝东边坐着读。"

小和尚照老和尚的话去做,背对着太阳诵读经文。渐渐地他就忽略了时间的快慢。

第二天,他对老和尚说:"师傅,您真高明,这一转换方向,我就忘记了时间,心思都浸在这经文里了。"

老和尚说:"无论做什么事,只有把时间放在身后,才能做到全神贯注,达到一种忘我的境界。"

---

[1] monk n. 修道士,僧侣　　　　[2] neglect v. 忽视,疏忽

The Vixen[1] and the Lioness
雌狐与母狮

One morning when a vixen was taking her babies out of the lair, she saw a lioness and her cub.

"Why do you have only one child, dear dame?" asked the vixen. "Look at my healthy and numerous[2] children here, and imagine, if you are able, a proud mother should raise more children."

The lioness said calmly, "Yes, just look at that beautiful collection. What are they? Foxes! I've only one, but remember that one is a lion."

一天清早,雌狐狸带着她的孩子走出巢穴,看见了母狮子和她的孩子。

"为什么你只有一个孩子,夫人?"雌狐狸问,"看我这群健康的孩子,想像一下如果有能力,一个骄傲的妈妈应该多养一些孩子。"

母狮平静地说:"是呀,看看这漂亮的一大群,他们都是狐狸!我只有一个,可他毕竟是一头狮子。"

---

[1] vixen n. 雌狐, 坏心眼的女人　　　　　[2] numerous adj. 很多的, 数目众多的

Two Dogs

A faithful farmyard hound, who served his master well the whole year round. A long-lost friend espied with joy. She was the curly spaniel Toy, reclining on soft downy cushion[1] in window niche.

As if she were a sister he had found, he almost weeped for joy, and pinging, whining. Against the wall he scratched and scrambled, and wagged his tail and gamboled.

"Well, Toy dear, tell me how you fare since Master took you in, to live with him up there? Out here we often starve, you've not forgotten how; say, what's the job you're doing now?"

"It were wicked to complain," says Toy, "I'm sure I'm Master's only joy; I live in luxury[2] and rich; I eat and drink off silver plate, and play on Master's lap, and when that fancy's gone, the sofa and the floor are nice to roll upon. What's happening with you?"

"Me?" said the honest hound—his tail was hanging limp, his muzzle near the ground. "I'm just as used to cold, as when we both were younger—and hunger; and over Master's house still keeping guard, I sleep and drench with rain out yonder in the yard; and when I bark, I get a kick, or else the stick! But how did you on such good fortune fall, you, who are only weak and small, while I slave out my soul, and all in vain? Say, what's your job?"

"My job! That's good. Say that again!" Cried little Toy, "I walk on my hind paws."

---

[1] cushion n. 靠垫，坐垫   [2] luxury n. 奢侈，豪华

两只狗

一只踏实的看家狗，终年为主人辛勤工作。他碰到了失散多年的朋友，感到非常高兴。那是一只卷毛哈巴狗托利，她躺在窗口柔软的绒垫上。

就像找到了亲姐妹似的，看家狗高兴得几乎哭了起来。他倚在墙上低声哀鸣，乱抓乱爬，还摇着尾巴蹦来蹦去。

"喂，亲爱的托利，自从主人把你带进去和他住以后，你过得怎么样？我们在外面还是会经常挨饿，你应该没有忘记吧。说说，你现在都在做些什么呢？"

"诉苦是罪过啊，"托利答道，"我肯定自己是主人惟一的快乐。我的生活奢华而且富贵，吃喝都是用银制的盘子。我在主人的膝头上玩耍，要是玩腻了，就在沙发和地板上舒舒服服地打滚儿。你过得怎么样呢？"

"我？"踏实的看家狗说着，尾巴无力地低垂下来，嘴巴也贴近了地面，"我还是经常受冻，和我俩小的时候一样，还会挨饿，还是看守主人的房子。我睡在露天的院子里，任凭风吹雨打。我一叫就挨一脚，或者挨一棍子！但是为什么你的命就这么好呢？你又弱又小，而我干得精疲力竭，却白费力气？说一下，你的工作是什么？"

"我的工作？对的，你说得对。"托利叫道，"我用后腿走路！"

The Fox Beside an Ice-hole

One frosty[1] morning in December, a fox stood drinking at an ice-hole, in the cold. Meanwhile, by carelessness or chance, he let his brush's tip inside the water dip, of which the ice took hold. Well, that was no great harm; there was not much to mind; just one good pull, as soon as said, left, perhaps, a dozen hairs behind; then off, in silence dead, while folks are still abed! But could he spoil his tail—a tail so soft and downy, so fluffy[2] and ruddy-browny?

No! Better just wait! There was not a soul to see, before there was, who knew? There would come a thaw, may be; the hole would give, and the tail came free. He waited and waited; the tail got faster still in prison. See! The sun had risen. Now folks were on their legs, and sounds of voices rose. Oh, then, poor fox, got frightened. He tugged and twisted and tried! No use. The tail was fast; the fatal[3] grip had tightened. By luck, a wolf came up.

"Dear friend! Old chum! Papa! Do save me!" cried the fox, "It's just in time that you come!"

His trusty friend stood still, and set about it with a will. He chose a very simple way, he neatly gnawed[4] the tail away. Untailed, our foolish fox made off for home full stride, and thought himself in luck, that still he kept his hide.

[1] forsty adj. 结霜的，严寒的   [3] fatal adj. 致命的，命运注定的；重大的
[2] fluffy adj. 蓬松的，松软的   [4] gnaw v. 咬，啃，啮

冰窟边的狐狸

十二月里一个寒冷的清晨,狐狸站在一个冰窟窿处喝水。期间不知道是疏忽还是凑巧,狐狸的尾巴浸在水里被冻结住了。其实这本来没什么大问题,也不必太在意,只需一拉,一下子就能把尾巴拉出来,可能扯掉十几根毛而已,再趁大家都在睡觉,悄悄溜回家去就行了。然而,狐狸哪里舍得损坏他的尾巴——条那么柔软、那么蓬松而红艳的尾巴啊?

不行,最好还是等等! 又没有人看见,谁会知道呢? 也许冰很快就会融化,冰窟窿一解冻,尾巴就出来了。狐狸等啊等啊,尾巴却愈冻愈紧。瞧! 太阳升起来了,人们开始忙碌了,周围响起了说话声。噢,这时候,可怜的狐狸害怕起来了。他又拉又扭,拼命挣扎! 没有用,尾巴动不了了,冰窟窿牢牢地冻住了尾巴。幸运的是,一只狼恰好过来了。

"亲爱的朋友! 老朋友! 干爸爸! 救救我吧!"狐狸喊道,"你来得正巧!"

他可靠的朋友停了下来,决心救救狐狸。狼采取了一个简单的方法,他干脆利落地咬掉了狐狸的尾巴。我们可怜的狐狸,没了尾巴,飞快地跑回家去,还庆幸自己走运,保全了狐皮呢。